W9-BHR-140

Dr. An Wang

Dr. An Wang

Computer Pioneer

By Jim Hargrove

Consultant: Parris H. Chang, Ph.D.
Professor of Political Science
Director, Center for East Asian Studies
The Pennsylvania State University
University Park, Pennsylvania

CHILDRENS PRESS®
CHICAGO

ACKNOWLEDGMENTS

Quotations used in this book from *Lessons* by Dr. An Wang with Eugene Linden, (Reading, Massachusetts: Addison-Wesley Publishing Company, Inc., 1986) are reprinted with permission courtesy of Boston University. Material from *The Boston Glove* reprinted courtesy of *The Boston Globe.*

PICTURE ACKNOWLEDGMENTS

AP/Wide World Photos — pages 56 (bottom right), 59 (top), 60 (top), 100 (bottom)

Black Star — © Rick Friedman, 4, 8

Permission Courtesy of Boston University — pages 28, 55 (4 photos), 56 (top and bottom left), 57 (3 photos), 118

Courtesy Hewlett-Packard Company — 59 (bottom)

SYGMA — © T. Orban, 60 (bottom)

UPI/Bettmann Newsphotos — pages 58 (3 photos), 98, 100 (top)

Cover illustration by Len W. Meents

Project Editor: Mary Reidy
Designer: Karen A. Yops

Library of Congress Cataloging-in-Publication Data

Hargrove, Jim.
   Dr. An Wang: computer pioneer/by Jim Hargrove.
   p. cm. — (People of distinction)
   Includes bibliographical references and index.
   Summary: A biography of the Chinese American computer pioneer and entrepreneur whose electronic calculator and word processor revolutionized the business world.
ISBN 0-516-03290-9
   1. Wang, An, 1920 — Biography — Juvenile literature [1. Wang, An, 1920-1990. 2. Computers — Biography. 3. Inventors. 4. Businessmen. 5. Chinese Americans — Biography. 6. Wang Laboratories, Inc.] I. Title. II. Title: Doctor An Wang. III. Series: People of distinction biographies.
QA76.2.W35H37   1993
338.7'61004'092 — dc20
[B]   92-35061
                                           CIP

TABLE OF CONTENTS

Chapter 1
Wang Laboratories   9

Chapter 2
Shanghai   15

Chapter 3
A Breakthrough at Harvard   29

Chapter 4
The Little Company That Could   43

Chapter 5
Meetings with the Giant   61

Chapter 6
A Calculated Move   73

Chapter 7
New Directions   87

Chapter 8
The Word Is Wang!   99

Chapter 9
The Empire Strikes Back   109

Notes   116

Time Line   118

Index   124

About the Author   128

Frederick Wang, board member and past president of Wang
Laboratories, and his father, An Wang

Chapter 1

WANG LABORATORIES

During its glory years in the 1970s and early 1980s, a company named Wang Laboratories changed the way businesses in America and much of the world worked with written words. Even more than such giant corporations as IBM (International Business Machines) and Xerox, Wang Labs shaped the modern job skill called word processing. Earlier, in the 1960s, the same company, with its line of innovative electronic calculators, revolutionized the way many business people worked with numbers.

By the mid-1980s, Wang products were in offices everywhere. At one point, more than 80 percent of America's largest two thousand corporations used computerized equipment from Wang Labs. By the start of the 1990s, however, all of that was changing with astonishing speed.

To a traveler driving along Route 128 in Lowell, Massachusetts, a suburb of Boston, it would not have been obvious that this giant corporation was struggling to survive. From the outside, the gleaming complex of huge, twelve-story buildings— the worldwide headquarters of Wang Laboratories—gave little hint at the trouble brewing within. But for the once mighty manufacturer, misery was becoming a way of life.

On July 25, 1991, a Wang official announced that his company had lost a staggering $314.5 million during the months of April, May, and June 1991. Like many other U.S. computer manufacturers in the summer of 1991, Wang Labs was suffering from a nearly worldwide business downturn. But for Wang, more than other high-technology firms, the bad news seemed without end.

Three months earlier, on April 24, Wang executives published a report filled with statistics that even then were becoming all too familiar. In the first three months of 1991, the report showed, Wang Laboratories lost nearly fifty million dollars. "We are not discouraged," Wang president Richard Miller told a *Boston Globe* newspaper reporter in April. "Fortunately, we saw the loss coming. We battened down the hatches in advance."[1] Miller knew what he was talking about. He, as well as other Wang presidents before him, had plenty of experience dealing with bad news about money. There was more to come.

Since 1985, Wang Laboratories had lost the kind of cash that brings to mind America's national debt. During another three-month period in 1989, the company lost $375 million. Total losses in a recent three-and-a-half-year period amounted to nearly $1.5 billion.

No company can lose that much money and survive for long. Between 1986 and the summer of 1991, Wang Labs was forced to let go of more than half of its total work force, from about

31,000 in 1986 down to 13,500 in 1991. Many of its best workers decided to leave on their own. The value of Wang's stock tumbled. Many experts wondered if the company would be able to survive much longer.

An end, of sorts, came in 1992. On August 28, Richard Miller announced that Wang Laboratories did not have enough money to pay its debts. In all, the company owed people and other businesses more than one-and-one-third billion dollars. Some debts were already long overdue. People were demanding to be paid. On that same day, Miller announced that his company was forced to declare bankruptcy. Now, the company's future would be in the hands of high-priced lawyers, accountants, and the people to whom Wang owed money.

On September 1, 1992 the accounting firm of Price Waterhouse, Inc. was selected to determine the remaining value of Wang Laboratories. Eventually, a bankruptcy court would decide whether to break up the firm or let it reorganize and stay in business. The decision would be based on which method would best allow the company to pay its bills.

If the company was broken up, everything it owned—from buildings to office chairs—would be sold to raise money to pay its debts. If it was reorganized, it would become just a pale shadow of its former self.

Just a few years ago, such a situation would have been hard to imagine. At that time, Wang Labs competed successfully with the largest computer firms on earth.

The once-giant firm was the result of one man's vision and hard work. He was born in China and came to the United States as a young man at the end of World War II. After earning a Ph.D. in physics at Harvard University, he went on to discover a form of magnetic memory that has been used in almost all computers for decades. In 1951 he started his own company, called Wang Laboratories, with a total investment of six hundred dollars. Although poor when he arrived in America, he became, by 1984, the fifth-richest person in the United States.

His name was Dr. An Wang. Until his death from throat cancer on March 24, 1990, Dr. Wang was one of the most highly respected computer pioneers in the world. Although it was not his primary interest, he also proved that he was a superb businessman. Despite his strongly competitive nature, he was a dedicated father and uncommonly generous with money.

A few years ago, Massachusetts Governor Michael Dukakis praised the Chinese-American inventor, both for his work with computers and for the millions of dollars in donations he gave to his adopted state. "I don't know how many countless thousands and thousands of people owe a debt of gratitude for what he did,"[2] Dukakis said. In 1986 President Ronald Reagan presented Dr. Wang with the Medal of Liberty, an award given to distinguished naturalized Americans. Two years later, he was inducted into the National Inventors Hall of Fame, a foundation established by the U.S. Department of Commerce.

During his lifetime Dr. Wang was awarded more than forty patents for his many inventions.

With the company he founded in such difficulty, it may seem as if the story of Dr. Wang's life must have a sad ending. But it isn't necessarily so. On June 18, 1991, officials from Wang Labs and IBM—once bitter rivals—made a stunning announcement. The two companies were forming a partnership to develop new computers. IBM—the world's largest manufacturer of computers—would make the hardware. Programmers at Wang Labs would help design it and create at least some of the software to make it work.

For An Wang, who died a little more than a year before the announcement was made, the news would have been unbelievable. In the highly competitive world of computer makers, no two companies battled more fiercely than Wang Labs and IBM. It was a business war that lasted throughout Dr. Wang's professional career. It was a war that An Wang eventually lost, but not before he had driven the corporate giant into a corner to battle for its life. Throughout the struggle, An Wang fought fairly. In the minds of many people, IBM did not.

Richard Miller, the current president of Wang Labs, summed up the life of the company's founder: "Dr. Wang's legacy is a life distinguished both as inventor and entrepreneur and as a good and decent man."[3] In the years following Dr. Wang's death, Miller and other Wang officials would continue the struggle to keep their company alive.

Frederick Wang, An Wang's older son, served as the president of Wang Labs for a while during the company's declining years. He still sits on its board of directors. In summer 1991, Frederick regarded IBM as a savior for his troubled company. Other industry experts were not so sure. After all, some pointed out, IBM had gained control of a multibillion-dollar corporation for a promise of payments somewhere between $25 million and $100 million.

A day after the deal was made, Frederick Wang summed up the matter with elegant simplicity. "Five years ago," he said, "the computer industry was a lot different than it is now."4

Chapter 2

SHANGHAI

An Wang, the oldest of five children, was born in Shanghai, China, on February 7, 1920. His family moved three times by the time he was a teenager. At the time of his birth, the family lived in a two-story rented house in a compound that belonged to his mother's relatives.

An's father, Yin-lu Wang, was better educated than most Chinese people of the era. He had attended a university for a year before getting a job teaching English in a private school in the town of Kun San. Kun San was about thirty miles from Shanghai up the Yangtze River. Because his father's job was so far away, for the first six years of his life An saw his father mostly on weekends.

In Chinese, the name *An Wang* means "Peaceful King." Unfortunately, China was hardly a peaceful place at the time of his birth.

In 1911 a revolution led by Dr. Sun Yat-sen ended the rule of a line of emperors in China called the Ch'ing Dynasty. For thousands of years, China had been ruled by emperors from a number of different dynasties. With the authority once commanded by these leaders gone, many groups, some headed by local strongmen known as warlords, struggled for control of

China. But it was not only the Chinese who fought to control their land.

During the 1800s, large areas of China had been carved up by other nations into what were called "spheres of influence." England, France, Germany, Japan, Russia, and eventually the United States all claimed sizable areas, often in partnership with other countries. In their spheres of influence, foreign nations could build transportation systems and conduct business with little control by the Chinese government or private citizens.

The years from the time just before An Wang's birth until World War II have been called the Age of Confusion in China. In a book about his life called *Lessons*, Dr. Wang wrote, "I was born in the middle of what has been called the Age of Confusion—the struggle for the soul of China after centuries of medieval rule. The bloodshed of this struggle, and later the Japanese invasion of my homeland, disrupted every aspect of my childhood. It was a time of complete uncertainty, not just for me and my family but for the institutions and ideas that had previously defined China."[1]

Even at the time of An's birth, Shanghai was one of the world's largest cities. Shanghai is located near the delta of the Yangtze River. The Yangtze empties into the East China Sea, a part of the Pacific Ocean. Much of the shipping trade of China, the world's most populous nation, was and still is concentrated in Shanghai. The importance of the sprawling seaport near the city has even left a lasting impression on the English language. For years, sailors from European and some other nations faced the danger of being "shanghaied," or kidnapped, and forced to sail on a ship.

Foreign nations, determined to take some of China's wealth, understood that the key to controlling much of the Chinese mainland was in the port of Shanghai. "If you wanted to dominate China," Dr. Wang wrote, "you had to control Shanghai. This is one of the reasons the city was the site of almost perpetual conflict during my childhood."[2]

During the mid-1920s, a group of Chinese soldiers led by Chiang Kai-shek gradually lessened the power of the warlords. Among Chiang's followers were members of the *Kuomintang* (the Chinese Nationalist party) and members of the Communist party. Although Communists helped him come to power, Chiang repaid them with death sentences in 1927.

"Once Chiang had established control over the warlords," Dr. Wang remembered, "he no longer needed the Communists, and in April 1927, he turned against them after forming a secret alliance with the bankers and merchants of Shanghai. He used local underworld gangs—who were his allies—to round up and slaughter the Communist Party members in the city. It was episodes like this that caused the period to be called the Age of Confusion."[3]

A year before all this took place, the Wang family moved from Shanghai to Kun San, where An's father taught school.

The little town escaped much of the bloodshed raging in Shanghai. But even at the age of six, An remembered a frightened uncle who hid in the family home for six months. His uncle had been a friend of the Communists, and was afraid he would be tortured and killed by Nationalist soldiers. Fortunately, he was able to hide until the danger passed.

An's childhood home in Kun San was comfortable and well made. It looked much like a typical house in Europe or North America.

As a six-year-old, An was ready to attend school. But the private school where his father taught began with the third grade. "So I began my schooling as a third-grader," Dr. Wang wrote, "and for the rest of my education in China, I remained two years younger than my classmates."4 At first, the schoolwork was very difficult. But An soon found that he could keep up with the older children. "I managed to stay up with the third graders when I was 6 years old, but I'm not a very good student," he confessed. "I'm the kind of student that, when the time calls for it, I manage to pass."5 Later in life, however, An became a very good student indeed. In the meantime, math became his favorite subject. He also enjoyed learning English, which all students at the school were required to take, starting in the fourth grade.

Not all of his lessons were learned in school. At home, his father helped him study important works in Chinese literature. His grandmother, particularly, taught him about the ancient Chinese philosophy called *Confucianism*. In this complex system of thought, moderation, balance, and the golden rule are stressed as parts of a complete life. Much later, Dr. Wang depended on his early lessons about Confucianism to keep his balance in the often-uncertain world of business.

In elementary school, An's grades in math and science courses were excellent, but his other grades were not. To get into junior high school, he had to pass a written exam in all subjects. His parents urged him to remain in the sixth grade for another year, to try to improve his understanding of topics such as history and geography. But An decided to take the exam anyway, and he got the highest score! His parents gladly paid the high tuition for junior high.

Even at the new school, however, An's old ways continued. He did well in science and math courses, and poorly in everything else. More than once, he had to take makeup classes for subjects he had failed. At the same time, he spent hours out of the classroom reading books about Western scientists, including Galileo, Newton, and the scientist-artist Leonardo da Vinci.

An was in junior high school in 1931 when Japanese soldiers captured Manchuria, a part of northeastern China. At the same time, Japanese airplanes bombed Shanghai, where An would soon be attending high school. It was the start of a long military struggle between China and Japan.

"Talk of Japan now replaced the domestic struggles as the topic of the day," Dr. Wang wrote in his book. "As the newspapers reported on the daily maneuverings of the Japanese, politicians trooped through our school to give political lectures we were forced to attend. We also had to participate in mass rallies at which speakers would inflame the crowd against the Japanese, and occasionally the British. Between the ages of eight and twelve, I was forced to join about five rallies a year. Listening to these presumably stirring speeches, I became deeply disenchanted with politics. It seemed to me that the more eloquent the speaker, the less likely it was that he would practice what he preached. These compulsory meetings turned me against political activism, and I never became caught up in the political fervor of the time."6

At the age of thirteen, An was back in Shanghai. There, he attended Shanghai Provincial High School, which had one of the best academic reputations in China. Many of the schoolbooks he studied there were written in English. The new school was relatively convenient for An, because it was just a few blocks from his grandparents' house. He could live with his relatives while he continued his studies.

Unfortunately, soon after he entered, the entire school moved ten miles outside the Shanghai city limits. (Educators probably felt it was safer there.) From that time on, An became a boarding school student, living in a tiny room at the school and going home on holidays.

Some of the high school subjects were difficult. Some were made even harder by the fact that the textbooks were written in English. An resented that fact for some time, but later realized that his command of the English language eventually made it much easier to succeed in America. During his high school years, the one sports event that An played in was soccer. Because he was younger and smaller than his classmates, he was made goalie. For a time, he claimed, he was "really more of a target"7 than anything else. Eventually, however, he grew enough to become a full-fledged player on a university team. He also became a skilled table-tennis player.

At the age of sixteen, An was accepted by Chiao Tung (now called Jiao Tong) University in Shanghai, the same school his father had attended for a year. Because he had the highest test scores when he entered, he was named class president, a position he held for the next four years. In all of China, no school was more respected in the sciences than Chiao Tung University. An majored in electrical engineering and, in particular, electronic communications. He felt the subject best matched his love of math and physics.

During his career as a university student in China, bad news seemed to come almost constantly. In 1936 An received word that his mother, whose health had been deteriorating for years, had died in Kun San. An always felt that his mother's strength had been exhausted by years of worry about the conditions her family faced in China. He felt that she was a victim of the Age of Confusion, as much as those who were killed in street fighting.

The following year, the dispute between Japan and China broke out into full-fledged war. Japanese soldiers seized the city of Beijing and, in a separate front launched in August, attacked Shanghai and marched westward toward Nanking, which was then China's capital.

Divided between Nationalists, Communists, remnants of the warlords, and still more factions, the Chinese army was no match against the well-armed, well-organized Japanese soldiers. One by one, villages and cities fell under the control of Japanese troops.

During the summer of 1937, An was staying at his father's house in Kun San. He had just completed his freshman year at Chiao Tung University. As news of the Japanese attack of Shanghai began to reach them, An and his father discussed what should be done. They decided that An should return quickly to the university, before safe travel became impossible.

An arrived at the campus without running into serious problems. But fully half his classmates were not able to cross the Japanese lines and return to the university on time for the start of classes. With the Japanese quickly taking over Shanghai, it seemed that it would no longer be possible to get any kind of normal education at Chiao Tung University. For the next several years, however, an odd quirk of fate allowed An to continue his studies in a relatively peaceful setting.

For nearly a century, the city of Shanghai was divided into Chinese and foreign sections. The old idea of the spheres of influence for foreign powers was still very much alive in the huge metropolis. Part of the city, an area of nine square miles, was called the foreign concessions. Within it were the French concession, run by French people, and the International Settlement, administered by British, American, and other foreign powers.

Both the French concession and the International Settlement came into being after British and Chinese soldiers fought in a disgusting conflict in the mid-1800s called the Opium War. Back then, the British felt they had the right to sell opium, a narcotic drug, to the Chinese people. When the Chinese government objected to England's "Just-Say-Yes-to-Opium" policy, British soldiers fought and won the right to push the drug. Among other concessions, the Chinese gave away part of Shanghai as well as the island and mainland territory known as Hong Kong.

For generations, the people of Shanghai and all of China resented the presence of foreign concessions in their own land. But in 1937 these territories suddenly became quite useful. Already at war with China, the government of Japan was not prepared for warfare with France, Great Britain, or the United States. For several years Japanese soldiers stayed out of the Chinese territories controlled by those nations.

Soon after the invasion of Shanghai, Chiao Tung University moved into a group of buildings inside the French concession. There, students and teachers were safe from Japanese soldiers.

"Thus, there was war all around me," Dr. Wang wrote much later, "but not in the nine square miles within which I spent the next three years. We could hear Japanese shells whistling overhead from time to time, but even though the war was close by, it was not there, and that made all the difference in the world. I could not venture beyond the concession without falling into the hands of the Japanese, but nine square miles is large enough so that this confinement was not a hardship."8 He was overjoyed when he learned that his family had managed to enter the safety of the Shanghai concession.

An continued his electrical engineering studies for the next several years. During that time, life in China became increasingly difficult. In 1939 World War II began in Europe as Germany began invading nation after nation. France was conquered in 1940. Its hold on the French concession in Shanghai was broken. Japan, allied with Germany throughout the war, took more and more control of the former French territory. In December 1941 Japanese airplanes attacked the U.S. military base at Pearl Harbor, Hawaii. The Japanese government was now at war with all the nations formerly in control of the International Settlement in Shanghai. No safe haven was left for Chinese citizens seeking to escape the rule of Japanese soldiers.

With nowhere to go after his graduation in 1940, An taught for a year at Chiao Tung University. Even by the summer of 1941, however, it was clear that the Japanese soon would be dominating all of Shanghai. An decided to leave the doomed concessions. At the same time, he found a way to help his country defend itself against the Japanese.

A group of people from the university was organizing a project to build radio transmitters for use by Chinese soldiers. It would be impossible to start such a venture in Shanghai without attracting the attention of the Japanese. The engineers decided to sneak away from Shanghai to the city of Kweilin. Far to the southwest of Shanghai, Kweilin was safe from Japanese soldiers traveling on foot. In a mountainous area with many caves, it would also provide natural shelters from bombing raids.

Traveling at night, An's group managed to pass the thinly stretched line of Japanese troops near the seacoast. Then they traveled on by steamboat and train to Kweilin. As soon as he arrived, An became the supervisor of a group of people building radios.

"We were never certain which radio parts would be available," he explained, "or when we would be stymied by a shortage of critical components. For instance, we had to invent a hand-powered generator to run a mobile radio transmitter needed by the troops. Because different people would turn the handles that powered the generator at different rates, we also had to invent a way of ensuring that the voltage was constant no matter how fast the handles were cranked. We got a lot of practice in the scavenging and improvisation that you often have to do when you're trying to design some new machine."9

An was working to help the Chinese army, but his experiences in Kweilin left him with bitter memories about the generals who led it. "The area around Kweilin was poor," he wrote, "and even the war with Japan did not keep corrupt military men and provincial officials from squeezing people to the point of starvation. As the war went on, the discipline of the armies broke down, and the generals became ever more openly outrageous in the way they treated their own people. After hearing of the atrocities committed by the Japanese, it was doubly disheartening to me to see the treatment my fellow Chinese were receiving from the troops supposedly there to protect them."10

As World War II raged on, bad news for An Wang continued to come like a charging army. Soon after he left Shanghai, as he eventually learned, his father had been killed. He was never able to discover the exact circumstances, only that his father's death was related to the war. One of his sisters died a few years later as well.

Throughout much of 1944, Japanese ground troops were slowly advancing toward Kweilin. Bombing raids had been a fact of life in the city for years. When the air-raid sirens went off, An and his assistants rushed to nearby mountain caves, where they played cards until the explosions ended.

Near the end of his stay in Kweilin, An took a written exam for an exciting new program sponsored by the Chinese Nationalist government and some Americans. A group of Chinese scientists and engineers would be chosen to study in the United States, where they could learn new techniques to help rebuild China after the war. An placed second in the test, and was soon accepted into the program.

In his book An notes that the Nationalist government of China soon paid for the bad behavior of its army. After World War II ended, battles continued within China. Communist soldiers led by Mao Zedong fought against Nationalist soldiers for control of the nation. By 1949 the Communists won a total victory. Many Chinese people were unwilling to help the Nationalist generals who had treated them so badly during the war with Japan.

With both of his parents dead and no family yet of his own, there was little to keep An in China. He made up his mind to go to America!

An Wang as a student at Harvard

Chapter 3

A BREAKTHROUGH AT HARVARD

An Wang and about ten other Chinese engineers flew in a DC-3 airplane over the Himalaya mountains from China to India in April 1945. Japanese soldiers were still in China, and so the flight, the first for most of the passengers, was a nervous one. The plane landed in northern India. From there, the engineers rode by train to Calcutta. It took a month for additional travel arrangements to be made. During his stay in India, Wang noted that conditions for poor people in Calcutta were the worst he had ever seen.

In early May Germany surrendered, ending the European battles of World War II. A few weeks later, Wang and the other engineers were aboard a ship passing through the Suez Canal, which had just been opened following the end of the fighting. The ship arrived in Newport News, Virginia, in June.

"When I arrived in the United States, I did not have any idea what I would be doing during my two-year visit," Wang wrote. "But although America was different, it did not present the dangers of the China I had left. It was unlikely that I would be bombed in the United States. I also knew that I would be doing something in a technical field, and science is the same the world over — a language I *could* speak."[1]

As part of the Chinese-American program, An was given $100 each month. It was not much money to live on, but because of it he knew he could survive in the new land.

For several weeks, most of the Chinese engineers lived on the campus of Georgetown University in Washington, D.C. Americans everywhere were still celebrating the end of the European battles of World War II. In August the war with Japan would end as well. But even with the great conflict nearly over, millions of young adults were still in the armed forces. That fact led to a fortunate break for An Wang.

When he left China, Wang thought he would find a job working for an American high-tech company. He did not even bring his school records from Shanghai. Now, however, he began to feel that he might continue his education at a university. With so many college-aged people in uniform, American universities found it difficult to attract their usual numbers of qualified students.

America's oldest college, still considered one of the world's best, is Harvard University, located in and around the cities of Cambridge and Boston in Massachusetts. In the closing months of World War II even Harvard was having trouble finding the kind of students it preferred to admit.

Wang applied to Harvard in the summer of 1945. Several teachers from Chiao Tung University had studied there in earlier years. Harvard officials probably knew the reputation of the Chinese school, and also may have known about the

Chinese-American program Wang had joined. At any rate, An Wang was quickly accepted by the department of applied physics at Harvard. He moved into Perkins Hall, a dormitory near the Law School, in September 1945.

Wang already had a college degree from Chiao Tung. The work he would be doing at Harvard was for an advanced degree: the most common are the master's degree and doctorate, or Ph.D. A scholar studying for these advanced degrees is called a postgraduate student or, more simply, a graduate student.

Wang began his postgraduate work at Harvard in the fall of 1945, when he was twenty-five years old. For a time the young graduate student was worried that work at Harvard, all conducted in English, might be difficult. In a matter of weeks his fears vanished. His English, although sometimes slow and hard to understand, was correct. He soon discovered that his years of building radios from available parts in Kweilin gave him practical knowledge in electronics that many American students lacked.

"In two semesters," he wrote, "I satisfied the requirements for a master's degree in applied physics. My first term, my grades were two A+'s and two A's. It put to rest any doubts Harvard might have had about my ability to handle the work."2

Wang completed work for his master's degree in less than a year. Unfortunately, at the time his studies were finished, his meager funding from the Chinese government began to disappear. China was being torn apart in a civil war fought between troops of the Nationalist government and Communist soldiers. In November 1946 An took a trip to Ottawa, Canada, where he worked as a clerk buying materials for the Chinese Nationalist government.

The boring nature of his job, as well as the approaching cold of a Canadian winter, made Wang quickly decide that he had made a mistake. Within weeks after arriving in Ottawa he wrote a letter to Professor E. Leon Chaffee, head of Harvard's Department of Applied Physics. In the letter he asked to be enrolled in the school's Ph.D. program.

The Harvard professor was aware of Wang's superb work as a master's student. He quickly accepted him into the Ph.D. program and even offered a part-time job as a laboratory instructor. Payment was $1000 a year, out of which Wang would have to pay his tuition, buy his books, and pay for all his living expenses.

"Even before returning to Cambridge," he wrote, "I vowed that if I was going to get my PhD, I was going to do it quickly. To be honest, I had little choice: with only a thousand dollars to pay my tuition and living expenses, I could just barely scrape by. The situation improved the following September when Dr. Chaffee recommended me for a Benrus Time Fellowship. This stipend allowed me to stop teaching and devote all my time to my PhD program."[3]

He did not need much time. Fewer than sixteen months

after starting the program, he earned his Ph.D. An Wang was now a doctor of applied physics, with a degree from one of the most famous universities in the world. Dr. An Wang, as he would be known now, soon found that a Harvard degree opened many doors. He needed the opportunities Harvard provided. International news stories led Dr. Wang and other Chinese-American scholars at Harvard to understand that Communist soldiers under Mao Zedong would soon conquer China. Dr. Wang, and about half his fellow Chinese students at Harvard, decided to stay in the United States.

The first of many doors that his Harvard education opened was at Harvard itself. For years Harvard scientists, engineers, and mathematicians had been working on early computers. The Harvard Computation Laboratory, directed by Dr. Howard Aiken, had been established to further the development of computers. Dr. An Wang soon played a pivotal role in the pioneering work done in that laboratory.

Throughout the early years of World War II Dr. Howard Aiken and a team of researchers from IBM had worked to develop a huge machine called the Automatic Sequence Controlled Calculator. It was nicknamed the Mark I. In 1944 the completed Mark I was moved to Harvard University. There, it was immediately pressed into service in America's war effort. Running twenty-four hours a day, the calculator first developed mathematical firing tables for the huge guns aboard U.S. navy ships. It also was used to test final formulas for the atomic bomb. Dr. Wang came to the Harvard Computation Laboratory after World War II, so he, of course, had no role in the Mark I's war-related activities.

The Mark I was perhaps the most powerful computer in existence during the last two years of World War II. But it was vastly different from today's small, electronic computers. At the heart of modern computers are thousands, often even millions, of tiny switches that can be turned on and off. In general, the switches have two purposes: first, to make a series of simple calculations, second, to store results of calculations or other bits of information. As in a modern computer, electrical switches were at the heart of the Mark I, but they were not tiny, and they operated under a different principle.

In today's integrated circuits, sometimes called *computer chips*, as many as a million tiny switches are turned on and off solely by the movement of electrons—or electricity. The switches are so tiny they can be seen only with a microscope. In the Mark I, the switches were much larger, each one about the size of a child's fist. Electric-powered magnets and metal springs were used to turn each switch on and off. Because it had many such switches and other parts, this early computer was nearly as large as a railroad car.

By today's standards, the Mark I was a very slow computer. It was also quite noisy. Dr. Wang noted that when the Mark I was operating, its switches made so much noise that it was difficult to carry on a conversation near it. Nevertheless, the

Mark I was a miracle of the mid-1940s. It could solve complex mathematical problems in a few seconds that would take trained mathematicians hours or even days to complete.

Dr. Howard Aiken was in charge of the Mark I and even newer computers at the Harvard Computation Lab. He was a tall, thin man whose sharp tongue was feared even by many of his closest coworkers. At the suggestion of Professor Chaffee, Dr. Wang approached Aiken about the possibility of working at the lab.

"Can you find a way to be useful?"[4] Aiken responded. Within a short time, Dr. Wang became astonishingly useful. But in the beginning, Dr. Howard Aiken took some getting used to.

"He was very strong willed," Dr. Wang said about his new boss, "and unpredictable even to those who had known him for a long time. I remember getting a ride with him on a number of occasions, and he was the kind of driver who had his foot either on the accelerator or on the brake the entire time—he never coasted. He put in extremely long hours, leaving the lab at eight or nine in the evening and returning sometimes as early as four in the morning. I don't think he ever met anyone . . . who he thought was smarter than he was. He was impatient with small talk, but that was never a problem with me. Because I was still grappling with the [English] language, I tried to be extremely concise when I spoke."[5]

Dr. An Wang was named a research fellow at the Harvard Computation Laboratory on July 1, 1948. The title was a mere formality. He was already working at the lab every day on a project Dr. Aiken had assigned to him. "He wanted me to find a way to record and read magnetically stored information without mechanical motion,"6 Dr. Wang wrote in his book.

Even by the summer of 1948, the problem of how to store information that a computer could read quickly had become the most troublesome part of the developing field. Two scientists at the University of Pennsylvania, John W. Mauchly and J. Presper Eckert, had shown in 1946 that vacuum tubes could be used to replace the electromechanical switches of the Mark I. In their ENIAC (Electronic Numerical Integrator and Computer), vacuum tubes by the thousands performed calculations much faster than moving switches, and could even be used to store information.

But the tubes had a number of problems. Like a light bulb, each one generated heat and would eventually burn out. Like the Mark I's switches, each was relatively large and expensive. The tubes also needed an uninterrupted supply of electricity. When ENIAC was turned off, all the bits of information stored in its thousands of vacuum tubes were lost.

By the late 1940s, pioneering computer scientists had developed many different ways to store information. All had drawbacks. The most simple solutions involved holes punched into paper tapes or cards. Each hole represented an on or off state of a single bit of information. Special machines were developed to "read" the holes and send the information to the computer processor. Compared to the speed at which the new computers could process the data, this procedure was extremely slow.

Another system involved storing bits of information as charges on magnetic tapes or on rotating magnetic drums. In some respects this system is similar to the disks in modern computers. With it, large amounts of information could be stored more or less permanently without requiring a steady source of electricity. This system was, and remains today, adequate for some aspects of computerized storage.

In one respect, however, storing magnetic information on moving tapes, drums, or disks was entirely unsatisfactory. To solve even the most simple problems, a computer's *central processing unit* (CPU) needs to be able to read and write stored information. Because the CPU operates extremely quickly, the stored information must be created and retrieved almost instantly. Otherwise, the CPU will spend nearly all of its time waiting for information.

The kind of memory used directly by the CPU during high-speed calculations is today called *random access memory*, or RAM. (*Read only memory* — or ROM — is similar. The only real difference is that ROM cannot be changed.) RAM and ROM devices are fast because they have no moving parts other than electrons, which pass through them at nearly the speed of light. Floppy disks, tapes, compact disks, and the like are sometimes called mass storage devices. The machines that use them include a number of mechanical parts that must move before information can be processed. They are, therefore, much slower than RAM devices. Before information from mass storage devices can be used by the CPU, it is usually necessary to copy the information into RAM. There, it can be read quickly by the CPU.

Even by the late 1940s relatively sophisticated mass storage devices were already in use. But the type of memory that came to be known as RAM was desperately in need of improvement. For a few years, vacuum tubes, despite the drawbacks already mentioned, seemed to provide the best solution. Other elaborate types of memory also were developed. Some were quite exotic. In mercury delay systems, patterns of tiny waves were formed in a tube filled with mercury, a very thick and heavy liquid at room temperature. The waves—the stored information—remained in motion long enough to be reused when the CPU needed to "remember" data it had stored. The system had many drawbacks, not the least of which was its expense. But it illustrates how hard computer scientists were working to find a way to store and read information quickly.

Dr. Howard Aiken, director of the Harvard Computation Lab, believed that magnetism offered the most promise for high-speed memory. He also was certain that any kind of mechanical movement would make the memory device too slow to keep up with a computer's CPU. He gave Dr. Wang the task of finding out how to use magnetism to store information without relying on moving parts. It was one of the most significant assignments in the history of computer science.

Dr. Wang began thinking about the problem he had been given. He knew that certain materials, including some forms of steel as well as iron and other minerals, become magnetized as electricity passes through them or near them. Some of these materials remain magnetic even after the flow of electricity has stopped. He also knew that depending on the direction in which the electricity flowed, a material could be magnetized in one of two different directions (called *fluxes*). Because the magnetic flux could exist in one of two states, it might be possible to replace the mechanical on-off switches of the Mark I and the troublesome vacuum tubes of ENIAC with small, simple magnets.

To store, or "write," a single bit of information, the CPU could send an electric current to the magnetic material. Depending on the direction of the current, the magnetic flux could be set to an "on" or "off" state. It also was possible to remember, or "read," the bit of information stored in the magnet by sending another electric current to it. If the current forced the magnet to change its flux, a small electrical pulse was created that could be read by the CPU. If the current did not cause a change in flux, no pulse was generated.

In this way magnetic flux could be used to both write and read information at high speed. There was, however, an enormous problem. Whenever the magnets were read by the CPU, the information they held was destroyed.

Dr. Wang wrestled with the problem for several weeks. In the meantime, he worked to improve the little magnets at the core of his new type of memory. He eventually decided to form the magnetic material into the shape of a tiny doughnut, called a *toroid*. He also searched for materials that would hold their magnetic flux for long periods without the application of electricity. Always, he grappled with the problem of preserving the magnetic information when it was read. At one point, he was ready to give up.

"But then one day while I was walking through Harvard Yard," he wrote, "an idea came to me in a flash. Like everybody else, I had been so preoccupied with preserving the magnetic flux as it was read that I had lost sight of the objective. I realized in that moment that it did not matter whether or not I destroyed the information while reading it. With the information I gained from reading the magnetic memory, I could simply *rewrite* the data immediately afterward. Moreover, since magnetic flux could be changed in a few thousandths of a second, I could do this without any real sacrifice of speed."7

The greatest problem faced by computer scientists of the day had been solved by Dr. An Wang. With his invention, soon called *core memory*, the basic problem of fast, small, inexpensive electronic storage had been solved. His new memory was included in the Mark IV computer.

One more breakthrough remained to be made. In Dr. Wang's

system, all the little magnets were placed along a single electrical path. To get even one bit of information, it was necessary to read all the data bits (magnet fluxes) in the computer's memory.

Dr. Jay W. Forrester, a computer scientist working at the Massachusetts Institute of Technology, took Dr. Wang's idea one step further. To understand Forrester's improvement, imagine a sheet of graph paper. Pretend that each line on the paper is an electric wire. Think of a little toroid magnet placed at each spot where one line, or wire, crosses another. This is the way Dr. Forrester wired together the memory cores invented by An Wang. The arrangement is called a *matrix*.

Because of his matrix wiring, Dr. Forrester was able to read a single bit of information without having to read any other. To do so, he applied half the amount of current needed to change a magnet's flux to each of two wires. At the exact spot where the two wires met, but at no other place, the current was great enough to read or write a bit of magnetic information. Random access memory, RAM, as we understand it today, was born. In this system, one or more random bits of information can be written or read without disturbing any other data.

The core memory system invented by Drs. Wang and Forrester was used in most computers throughout the 1950s and 1960s. After that, these systems were gradually replaced by on-off switches built into silicon microcircuits, or chips. However, because magnetic core memory is sturdy and holds its information even when electric currents are turned off, some core memories are still used today. The shuttle spacecrafts used by NASA, for example, include backup computers with this type of memory.

Chapter 4

THE LITTLE COMPANY THAT COULD

Dr. Wang was still in the early stages of his work on memory cores when he met the young woman who soon became his wife. Her name was Lorraine Chiu. Like her future husband, Lorraine had been born in Shanghai. In the huge Asian city, it is hardly surprising that the two had never met. Her English first name came from the fact that other members of her family had lived in the United States. Both her parents were born in Hawaii and later moved to China. Lorraine came to the United States to study English literature at Wellesley College near Harvard. In 1948, the two met at a party for Chinese students studying in the Boston area.

An and Lorraine enjoyed each other's company. They began dating, and in 1949 they decided to get married. Unfortunately, China's civil war was in its final stages at the time. It was impossible, therefore, for the two to travel to their homeland. The normal Chinese custom called for them to seek the approval of Lorraine's parents before being married. With some sadness, the couple knew it was impossible to follow the tradition. After their marriage in 1949, they moved into an apartment in Cambridge.

The same year he was married, Dr. Wang decided to try to

patent his invention of memory cores. A patent—a legal document issued by the government—gives an inventor certain rights over the use of his invention. A successful patent usually means that an inventor is entitled to receive money each time his invention is used. In the case of an important discovery such as core memory, a patent can be worth a fortune.

Obtaining a patent, however, is a complex project. Although An filed the first papers for core memory with the U.S. Patent Office in October 1949, he was not awarded a patent until many years later.

In the meantime, Dr. Wang worried about how his boss would react to his application. Perhaps out of fear of Howard Aiken's legendary temper, no one else at the Harvard Computation Lab had applied for a patent, at least none that Dr. Wang could find. Despite his fears, he knew that he had to inform his boss of his actions.

"It turned out that my apprehension was groundless," Dr. Wang wrote. "I could hardly say that Dr. Aiken was overjoyed with my news, but he showed no negative reaction. In fact, he did not react at all. Later he gave me another substantial raise, which I took to mean that he was not too put out by my actions. In any event, there was no noticeable difference in our relationship in the year and a half I spent at the lab after our conversation."[1]

During his final eighteen months at Harvard, Dr. Wang continued working on the Computation Lab's newest computer, the Mark IV. Meanwhile, developments in computer science were taking place at breathtaking speed.

During the late 1940s, a Hungarian-born mathematician named John von Neumann devised what is now called the *stored-program technique* of computer control. Until von Neumann changed everything, early computers had to be wired by hand to solve various problems. This process often involved setting hundreds of switches and/or plugging scores of wires into the appropriate receptacles. These complex procedures made computers ready to solve a particular type of problem.

Von Neumann showed that this "wiring" could be done with coded information. In his stored program, all the known information about a problem, as well as the instructions for solving that problem, was sent to a computer's memory.

The world's first stored-program computer, EDSAC (Electronic Discrete Sequential Automatic Computer), was completed at Cambridge University in England in 1949. Other stored-program computers were quick to follow. The most famous early model was UNIVAC (Universal Automatic Computer), built by John W. Mauchly and J. Presper Eckert of the University of Pennsylvania. The first UNIVAC was installed at the U.S. Census Bureau in early 1951, where it was run night and day for a decade.

UNIVAC included a number of startling innovations. It was the first computer designed to be built in quantity. Before it was phased out for more advanced models, forty-seven UNIVACs were built. UNIVAC was also the first computer to process words as well as numbers. It accomplished this by assigning numeric codes to each letter of the alphabet and to punctuation marks as well.

The development of what was soon called core memory by Drs. Wang and Forrester attracted considerable attention from computer scientists. It was clear now that compact, fast, reliable memories could be produced more inexpensively than ever before. The invention made it possible for computers to have larger memories—big enough to store programs as well as raw data and results. By the early 1950s, many people were beginning to realize that computers might soon change the world.

It was clear to Dr. An Wang and to others at the Harvard lab that computers could be made and sold for a profit. At the time, Harvard had a policy not to emphasize research that could also be carried on by businesses and corporations to make money. Dr. Wang realized that the university was about to abandon its basic research in computer science.

During the spring of 1951 An began thinking about going into business for himself. He read books and articles about small businesses and weighed the pros and cons of the move. He knew he would be giving up a steady salary of fifty-four hundred dollars a year, not bad for a young man at the time. But money was a concern. Lorraine had already given birth to their first son, Frederick, in September 1950. An would have to use his savings of about six hundred dollars to support his growing family until he began earning money from his new business.

On the other hand, Dr. Wang was one of the world's leading experts on computer memory. Papers he had published in scholarly magazines had attracted much interest from other computer scientists. If he formed a small company to build core memories for larger companies building and experimenting with computers, he might be able to survive.

In April Wang submitted his resignation to Howard Aiken, effective in June. At about the same time he traveled to Boston's City Hall to fill out a form and pay a small registration fee to form a type of small company known as a sole proprietorship. He named his new company Wang Laboratories. At the time its value was approximately nothing. Thirty-five years later Wang Laboratories would be worth in the neighborhood of ten billion dollars.

From the very beginning Americans tended to pronounce incorrectly both Dr. Wang's last name and the name of his new company. When An came to America in 1945, he could not make an exact English translation of his Chinese name. Although the English spelling makes it seem that his name should rhyme with "sang," a closer rhyme is really "song." Perhaps his name should have been spelled Wong.

Even in 1951 he had already given up trying to correct the

way Americans spoke his name. "Let the country decide how they want to pronounce it," he told a newspaper reporter in 1983. "My perception is that you can't get 200 million people to pronounce it the way you want it."2

The name he chose had particular significance. Throughout its glory years in the 1970s and early 1980s, Wang Laboratories was, above all else, a family company. An Wang and his family held onto control of the growing business throughout its founder's life. An chose the plural form, "laboratories," in the hope that his enterprise would grow over the years. That wish came true beyond his wildest dreams.

In June 1951 Dr. Wang rented a tiny second-floor office at 296 Columbus Avenue in Boston's South End. The little brick building housing his dingy office was attached to the end of a block of row houses. The cost, unfurnished, was seventy dollars a month. Out of his six-hundred-dollar savings, An purchased a chair and a table, and he had a telephone installed. He also printed a one-page flier describing his new business.

While still at the Harvard Computation Lab, Dr. Wang had researched the best materials to use in his doughnut-shaped magnetic memory cores. Eventually, he found a material made out of nickel and iron that a United States company was selling under the trade name Deltamax. Although this alloy would soon be replaced in core memories by substances called *ferrites*, at the time Deltamax was the best-known material to make toroids for core memories. Dr. Wang began looking for people and organizations who might be interested in buying his Deltamax cores.

He started his marketing work by borrowing a book from the Harvard library that listed United States research laboratories. Thinking that scientists in those labs might need his core memories for their electronic projects, he began making telephone calls and sending out fliers. At the same time he decided how much to charge for his new devices.

To make the magnetic toroid that would store a single bit of memory in a computer, all he had to do was get Deltamax from the supplier, a company called Allegheny Ludlum Steel, and wrap the substance with electric wire, a procedure that required only a soldering gun. He decided that he could sell each core for four dollars and still make a profit.

As he soon learned, many people in the early 1950s were willing to pay that price for a single bit of computer memory. Today, such a price would be unthinkable. By 1991 a single computer RAM chip able to store one million bits of information could be purchased for about five dollars. Thirty years earlier, Dr. An Wang would have priced a similar amount of core memory at four *million* dollars. In other words, in thirty years, the cost of computer memory fell to nearly one one-millionth of its 1951 price. But despite costs of nearly a million times higher than today, Dr. Wang soon found a market for his invention. In 1980, he summed up three decades of experience in making and buying components for computers: "The cost of parts keeps getting lower," he noted, "and the applications are getting wider."3

Toward the end of his first month in business, Dr. Wang began to get responses to his phone calls and letters. "At first, it would be a big day if an order came in for four memory cores," he wrote. "Lorraine remembers that I would come home and say, 'We got an order for four cores today!' as though this were particularly good news. In fact, it was."4 At the same time, Dr. Wang began working on new inventions.

An Wang was working in the relatively new field called *digital electronics*. The word "digital" referred to the units of electric pulses whose existence or nonexistence could represent digits, or *bits*, in the binary numbering system (the base-two system whose only digits are 0 and 1). Small groups of bits, called *bytes*, could stand for digits in other numbering systems, including our familiar base-ten system, as well as individual letters of the alphabet and special codes used by the computer processor.

At the time only true computers—huge and tremendously expensive—were able to manipulate digital data. But many electronics experts all over the world were suddenly feeling the need for digital machines that were not as complex as a full-fledged computer. Dr. Wang set to work developing a simpler machine that could count, store, and display digital data. Today, such a device is called a *digital counter*. From the simple counter, An designed a number of other machines that, although they used some of the principles of digital computers, were smaller, simpler, and far less expensive.

For example, he developed a digital tachometer, a little instrument that measures the rotational speed of an engine in a car or truck. He even designed a counter that could be used in nuclear laboratories to measure the way radioactive materials behaved. He had so many ideas that it was impossible for him to find the time to develop them all.

Before long Dr. Wang hired an assistant, an advertising art student from Boston University named Bob Gallo. For fifty-five cents an hour, Gallo helped assemble Deltamax cores, designed the company's logo (at a total cost of less than three dollars), and greeted visitors. He was soon surprised to see high-ranking military officials arrive at the office door. America's armed forces were becoming increasingly interested in computers.

Near the end of 1951 Dr. Wang and his assistant packed some core memories and a few digital devices into the back of Wang's ancient Buick and drove to New York City. There, they set up an exhibition booth at the Institute for Radio Engineering convention in Manhattan.

"The Wang booth (which consisted of a card table) saw a good deal of traffic during the convention," Dr. Wang wrote. "Bob's job was basically to keep the crowds of visitors happy until they could get a chance to talk with me. He had become adept at that from the hours he had spent entertaining the generals and other officials who had come through the Boston office. I took it as a good sign that my display attracted so much attention. There seemed to be a lot of curiosity about what I was doing. The convention produced a spurt of orders, and I decided to make a point of attending future conventions."5

From June through December 1951 Wang Laboratories earned $3,253.60, almost entirely through the sales of memory cores. With some satisfaction Dr. Wang noted that it was more than he had earned during the first half of the year at the Harvard Computation Lab. Still, the new company had expenses. He found it necessary to add to his income by giving lectures, twelve dollars per class, at Boston's Northeastern University. As orders began to increase he hired a second assistant, a Northeastern University student, to wind wires around the Deltamax toroids used in his memory cores.

By the following year, 1952, his work with digital counting devices began to pay off. An electronics lab in Cambridge hired him as a consultant to develop a specialized digital component. "This contract gave me a three-hundred-dollar-a week income," he wrote, "the first steady stream of income I'd had since I founded the company."6 Other projects involving digital devices followed.

Even at this early stage in his career, Dr. An Wang had developed many of the habits for which he would be known for decades. He usually dressed in a dark, two-piece suit, a white shirt, and a bow tie. His wife Lorraine quickly discovered that her husband had a habit of writing out electronic designs and notes to himself on any scrap of paper he could find.

"He probably has his work on his mind all the time," she said. "Because anytime he can take out a piece of paper and be scribbling on it, he does it. He makes notes to himself all the time. Sometimes in a restaurant, he'll be drawing something on a napkin."7

In his autobiography Dr. Wang explained his sometimes unusual work habits. "Some inventors are born tinkerers," he wrote, "who like nothing better than to play with electrical components all day long, and who maintain elaborate workshops at home so they can continue to work late into the night. This is not my style at all. I do most of my serious thinking with a pad of graph paper and a pencil. I am adept at tinkering when the occasion calls for it, but I do not need to have physical objects in my presence in order to work with them. To this day, I do not have a workshop in my home. Nor do I work in thirty-six-hour binges like most 'hackers.' If I have an idea in the evening, I am content to wait until the next day to see whether it works out in practice."8

Dr. Wang had to wait a few years to see his company begin its phenomenal growth. But he always seemed pleased that he had been able to start the giant enterprise on such a small scale. In 1971, a few years before Wang word processing computers became known throughout the world, he summed up his feelings about his humble start. "Those of us who were with the company for a long time learned about business by experience," he said, "but without the pressures of growth forcing us to become pure administrators. When growth came, I think we could handle it better."9

By the 1970s Dr. Wang and other officials with Wang Laboratories needed all the training and preparation they could get. It was then that Wang Labs began its business war with the world's largest computer manufacturer. But even in the 1950s, the first skirmishes had already begun.

An Wang's father, Yin-Lu Wang

An Wang's childhood home in Kun San

An Wang's mother, Z.W. Chien, and his aunt, Z.T. Chien, in the 1920s

A part of the six-hundred-year-old Wang family genealogy

An Wang with his sister Hsu Wang in 1940

Left: This photo shows An Wang when he was graduated from Chiao Tung University. Right: Dr. E. Leon Chaffee, head of Harvard's Department of Applied Physics, accepted An Wang at Harvard and offered him a part-time job.

Lorraine Chiu and An Wang were married on July 10, 1949.

Courtney and Fred Wang

An and Lorraine Wang's daughter Juliette

Above: Howard Aiken, inventor of the automatic sequence controlled calculator (Mark I), reads a tape from his machine in 1943. Below left: The ENIAC was built in 1946. The inventors, J. Presper Eckert, Jr. and John W. Mauchly, are standing in the foreground. This photo does not show the calculator's power source, which occupied about half as much space as the computer. Below right: In 1951 J. Presper Eckert sits at the controls of the UNIVAC and demonstrates how it will be able to sort data on citizens according to sex, ethnic background, marital status, age, education, and just about anything else the U.S. Census Bureau would like to know.

By the end of the twentieth century computers were being used by children in their classrooms.

The Hewlett-Packard Company produced a palmtop personal computer—a far cry from the ones that took up buildings. Comparisons between the HP 95LX and enormous old computers can be seen at the Computer Museum of Boston in Boston, Massachusetts.

Above: Harvard's Mark III was a ten-ton mechanical computer. Below: An Wang (fourth from right, with bow tie) is honored as a distinguished immigrant during Liberty Weekend in New York City in 1986.

Chapter 5

MEETINGS WITH THE GIANT

In the mid-1950s the Wangs purchased a ten-room house in the town of Lincoln, a suburb of Boston. Although the family's new home included more than twenty acres of land, it could hardly be described as a lavish mansion. Oddly, the Wangs never moved from the white clapboard house, even after Dr. Wang became one of the richest people in America. Friends and coworkers felt the home was too close to the highway for someone of his wealth, but he never gave in to suggestions to move.

For more than five years before he purchased his home, Dr. Wang was forced to spend considerable time defending and marketing his patent on magnetic memory cores, which he first applied for in October 1949. While the application was being studied—a process that took nine years—Dr. Wang still enjoyed some legal protection for his idea. Since patent papers had been filed, the memory core was protected under the term "patent pending," which meant that full protection was expected in the future. The effort to market his invention gave Dr. Wang his first inside look at the workings of IBM.

Today, IBM is by far the largest manufacturer of computers in the world. Its 1990 worldwide sales amounted to sixty-two billion dollars—more than the gross national products of Bolivia, Chile, and Egypt combined. Even in the early 1950s, just before it began selling computers, IBM was a huge corporation. It made electric typewriters, mechanical calculators, and other machines used in government and business offices. Yearly sales in the early 1950s amounted to hundreds of millions of dollars.

Shortly before he left the Harvard Computation Lab, Dr. Wang sent a letter to IBM asking if the company would be interested in purchasing a license to use his memory cores. He received the first of many letters from the corporation in June 1951, at about the same time he began Wang Laboratories. For a time IBM officials showed only mild interest in his invention. But before long, a steady stream of visitors from the company began to arrive at his little office on Columbus Avenue. Most seemed surprised to learn that Wang Labs was basically a one-man operation.

With a young lawyer named Martin Kirkpatrick, who had helped with his patent application, Dr. Wang discussed the invention with many people from IBM. In November 1953, after more than two years of talks, an agreement was finally made. Dr. Wang would be paid a thousand dollars a month to work part-time as a consultant, a hired expert, for IBM. At the same time, IBM received an option, lasting until February 1956, to purchase a license to use Dr. Wang's magnetic memory cores.

It was becoming increasingly obvious that Dr. Wang's invention, along with Jay W. Forrester's improvement using matrix wiring, was about to revolutionize all of computer science. Already, pioneers at Massachusetts Institute of Technology (MIT) had built a computer with a magnetic core memory thousands of times larger than in earlier machines. In the MIT computer, Dr. Wang's magnetic toroids were made out of the compound called *ferrite*. The ferrite memory cores were arranged in what is known as a *three-dimensional matrix*.

In an earlier chapter of this book, a simple, two-dimensional matrix was compared to a sheet of graph paper. A three-dimensional matrix can be thought about in much the same way. But instead of picturing just one sheet of graph paper with a memory core where each line intersects, imagine a pile of seventeen sheets of graph paper. Think of lines, symbolizing electrical wires, passing straight through all seventeen sheets of paper. In the new MIT computer, a ferrite memory core was placed at the intersection of not two, but three different lines (wires). In the two-dimensional matrix, half the electric current needed to change the core's magnetic flux was allowed to flow in each of two wires. In the three-dimensional matrix, one-third of the necessary current was put in each of three wires. Even in this more complicated arrangement, a single core—a single bit of memory—could be read or written to without disturbing any other bit. In MIT's new three-dimensional matrix, it was possible to store more than seventeen thousand bits of information. In 1953, this amount of memory was unheard of. (Today, however, even small desktop computers have millions of bits of random access memory.)

IBM officials realized that ferrite memory cores, arranged in a matrix, were the key ingredients in the new computers it was planning to build. However, a number of different people, including Wang and Forrester, had already applied for patents. If the applications were granted, IBM and other manufacturers would need permission to use the new invention. Of all the patent applications, Dr. Wang's was the oldest and the most critical. Strangely enough, IBM seemed in no hurry to come to an agreement. Even though the company was planning to use ferrite memory cores in new computers, discussions with Dr. Wang dragged on and on.

On May 17, 1955, the U.S. Patent Office formally issued Patent Number 2,708,722 to Dr. An Wang for the invention of magnetic memory cores. As with all new patents, there would be a one-year period in which other inventors could challenge the patent by declaring an "interference." If someone else could prove an earlier claim to the invention, the patent could be taken back, or at least changed. However, Dr. Wang and his lawyers had carefully studied patent records and were confident that no significant challenge would be raised.

In fall 1955, after the patent had been issued, IBM officials and Dr. Wang and his lawyers were still discussing licensing terms. In October, IBM offered to buy the patent outright for half a million dollars plus some additional payments when other manufacturers used memory cores. At the same time, the offer included words indicating that much of the money would have to be returned to IBM if another inventor could prove an "interference" with the patent. Dr. Wang refused to accept the offer.

It was clear that IBM executives had finally realized the true importance of Dr. Wang's invention. During earlier stages of the talks, IBM people suggested payment of one cent for each bit of core memory they used. Now, they realized, such a payment schedule might well amount to millions of dollars within a few years.

In the closing months of 1955 time was running out for IBM. The company's option to buy a license for memory cores would end in February. At the same time, the one-year period for other inventors to challenge Dr. Wang's patent would expire in May. The giant office machine company continued the talks with renewed intensity.

IBM presented Dr. Wang with several lengthy lists of questions he was expected to answer before another offer would be made. Dr. Wang suspected that many of the questions might be attempts to loosen his grip on the patent he had just been given. Did Howard Aiken of Harvard Computation Labs own part of the invention? Had not other computer pioneers thought about using magnetic flux to store data? The questions went on and on. Dr. Wang did his best to answer each one. Martin

Kirkpatrick talked to a number of computer scientists, including those Dr. Wang had worked with. He could find no evidence indicating the invention belonged to anyone else.

By the early days of 1956 the inventor expected an agreement to be made quickly. IBM's option on the memory cores would end the following month. No serious challenges to his patent had been made.

"Once again," Dr. Wang wrote, "IBM had some surprises in store for us. In early January, they pointed out a forgotten clause in our agreement that gave them four months after the expiration of the option to come to an agreement to buy the patent. Simultaneously we were informed that despite this clause, IBM was willing to come to an immediate agreement. Shortly after this . . . IBM revealed its thunderbolt."[1]

A lawyer for the corporation announced that IBM had discovered a Los Angeles city worker, Frederick W. Viehe, who was about to claim an "interference" with Dr. Wang's patent. At the same time the IBM lawyer said that he could not discuss the details of the complaint.

Suddenly, Wang's patent seemed in danger. Oddly, IBM announced that despite the new threat, it was willing to come to an immediate agreement to buy the patent. Dr. Wang felt he had little choice but to agree. Defending his invention against the new attack would take a great deal of time and money. He needed to spend more time working on new projects at Wang Labs.

On March 6, 1956, he signed a contract selling his patent for core memories to IBM for half a million dollars. The contract listed a number of conditions, including an interference claim, under which IBM could withhold payment of the final $100,000. That final sum was never paid.

Normally, when an invention is disputed, a series of meetings are held with Patent Office officials to determine the rightful owner. In November 1957, however, it was quietly announced that IBM had purchased Mr. Viehe's patent application. Because the company now owned the rights to both disputed patents, a full hearing was not necessary. Nevertheless, a quick ruling by Patent Office officials was in favor of Dr. Wang on fifteen of sixteen claims. Wang could certainly have won the sixteenth, which was awarded to Viehe on a technicality, but a long struggle was no longer required.

Frederick Viehe died a wealthy man in 1960. Before his death, he said only that he had sold the rights to an invention and was sworn to secrecy about all aspects of the sale. His son, however, later confirmed that IBM had been the purchaser. Dr. Wang suspected, but could not prove, that IBM officials had helped Frederick Viehe challenge his patent. Why else, Dr. Wang wondered, would they have sworn him to secrecy about the deal? Dr. Wang's patent was more technically advanced, but he had not been told to remain quiet. At any rate, Viehe's claim helped IBM drive down the price of Wang's invention.

Over the next few decades, the rights to Dr. Wang's invention were worth a fortune. With core memories now solidly in its corporate pockets, IBM quickly went on to become the largest computer manufacturer in the world.

An had misgivings about his deal with IBM. But the payment of $400,000 made him a relatively wealthy man, especially considering the value of mid-1950s dollars. The money helped him pay for his new home in Lincoln, which was purchased around the time the patent sale was finalized.

Nearly a year before he signed the final agreement with IBM, he and Lorraine became United States citizens. At the time, the Chinese government was threatening to demand the return of students who remained in the U.S. after the Communist takeover in China. Officials from the U.S. government invited An and his wife to become naturalized citizens. The ceremony took place on April 18, 1955.

Dr. Wang had mixed feelings about surrendering his Chinese citizenship. "While I disliked what was going on there politically," he wrote, "China was still my birthplace. Nor did I think that America was a utopia. Indeed, at this time, America was being swept away by the irrationality and paranoia of McCarthyism [an anti-Communist witch hunt led by U.S. Senator Joseph McCarthy]. Still, it seemed to me that America had the best system—as a nation we do not always live up to our ideals, but we have structures that allow us to correct our wrongs by means short of revolution."[2]

The middle and late 1950s was a period of rapid change for Wang Laboratories, and for the Wang family as well. Courtney, An and Lorraine's second son, was born. Even earlier, in 1955, Wang Labs became a corporation. An, Lorraine, and Martin Kirkpatrick served as the new corporation's board of directors. Like many other corporations, Wang Labs issued stock when it was formed. Some companies sell stock to other people as a way to raise money. Dr. Wang made sure that he and his family owned all the stock in Wang Labs. For more than three decades he worked hard to make sure that the majority of the company's controlling stock remained in his family's hands. Also during the 1950s Dr. Wang moved his little company several times, first to Cambridge and then to Natick, another town near Boston. By 1958, Wang Labs employed ten people.

During this same period, a relatively new device called the *transistor* began yet another revolution in the field of electronics. Until the mid-1950s, vacuum tubes, usually made of glass and metal and about the size of a fat pickle, were the fastest devices to control the flow of small amounts of electricity in an electronic circuit. The transistor, about the size of a large pea, was able to perform many of the functions of the larger vacuum tubes. Unlike the vacuum tube, however, most transistors did not develop large amounts of heat. Under heavy use, they were far less likely to burn out. Because of their small size and resistance to heat-related breakdowns, transistors rapidly began to replace tubes in many electronic devices.

At the same time that transistors began to be used commercially, engineers found a simple way to combine many of them in electronic circuits. On what were called *printed circuit boards*, wires connecting transistors and other small devices were replaced by metallic lines etched—or printed—directly on the surface of a card made of fiberglass or other materials. Printed circuits soon allowed complicated electronic instruments, including radios and televisions, to become much smaller. In a few more years, many printed circuit boards themselves were replaced by even smaller devices, today's integrated circuits, often called "chips."

Long before integrated circuits came into general use, Wang Labs began manufacturing printed circuit boards that performed many of the same functions now taken over by chips. Since these boards used digital electronics to perform specific calculations, they were sometimes called *logic cards*. Under a U.S. air force contract, Dr. Wang developed a printed circuit board that could help perform the mathematical calculations needed to measure the height of clouds near airports. The project gave him an idea.

"While working on the government's cloud-ceiling-measurement contract," he wrote, "I had gotten the idea that companies might like to buy the separate boards containing individual logic functions. With these boards, they could put together their own packages of digital electronics, customized to perform various functions. I called the boards Logiblocs, and sold them through contacts I had made in the course of my consulting work."3

Dr. Wang knew that logic cards could be used to control the movement of some factory machines. Using simple programs, either on paper tapes with holes punched in them or on magnetic tape, logic cards could translate binary information into electrical signals to control some machine functions. Under the brand name Weditrol (short for Wang Electronic Digital Control Units) the company was soon selling between sixty and eighty specialized printed circuit boards a year to industrial corporations. A little later, a similar device, along with some other circuits Dr. Wang developed, was used to drive one of the world's first outdoor digital scoreboards. It was installed at Shea Stadium, home of the New York Mets baseball team.

One of the corporations that purchased Weditrol printed circuit boards was the Warner & Swasey Company, a large machine tool manufacturer based in Cleveland. Looking for money to expand Wang Labs, Dr. Wang began a business relationship with Warner & Swasey that he eventually regarded as a mistake.

After a series of talks with officials from the Cleveland firm, an agreement was reached in the fall of 1959. Dr. James C. Hodge, executive vice president of Warner & Swasey, agreed to loan Wang Labs one hundred thousand dollars. At the same time, for another fifty thousand dollars, Warner & Swasey was awarded stock giving it a one-quarter ownership of Wang Labs.

In a matter of a few years Warner & Swasey's fifty-thousand-dollar investment was worth a hundred million dollars. It was so valuable that another company took over Warner & Swasey and paid for the entire purchase merely by selling a portion of the Wang Labs' stock.

In the meantime, An Wang knew that he had made a serious error. He had given away 25 percent of his company for far less than it was really worth. He vowed he would never make the same mistake again.

It was a wise decision. During the next decade, the 1960s, Wang Labs began the phenomenal growth that would eventually make the Wang family rich beyond even their wildest dreams.

Chapter 6

A CALCULATED MOVE

In the late 1950s computers were beginning to change the way people set type used to print the text in books, magazines, and newspapers. For the first time, typesetting machines were made that used a computer and a cathode ray screen. (Called a CRT for short, it was really a specialized vacuum tube similar to a television picture tube.)

One of the hardest parts of typesetting involved making both the right and the left margins even, as they are on the pages of this book. The process of increasing or decreasing the spaces between words and even individual letters so all lines on a page will end at the same right margin is called *justification*.

To make justified columns of type, it is often necessary to divide a word so that it begins at the end of one line and is completed at the start of a new line. A hyphen is placed where the word is broken at the end of the first line. The rules of grammar allow words to be divided only between syllables. To divide words automatically and accurately, therefore, computers had to store all or parts of hyphenating dictionaries of the English language in memory. This, of course, called for larger-than-ever core memories. Typesetting computers of the late

1950s cost the better part of a million dollars. Even though they used a CRT and were so expensive, these typesetting machines did not have the editing abilities of a simple word processor today. Often, the CRT was used primarily for displaying and justifying type after it had already been set on a typewriterlike machine.

Around the year 1960 the president of a little typesetting company in Cambridge, called Compugraphic, visited Dr. Wang. William Garth, Compugraphic's president, suggested that Wang Labs might be able to build a typesetting machine according to Compugraphic's specifications. Dr. Wang accepted the challenge. To keep the cost of the machine lower than competing models, Compugraphic and Wang Labs agreed to make hyphenation a manual operation. When a word needed to be divided, the computer would signal the operator, who would hyphenate the word by hand.

At the time Wang Labs employed about twenty people. During a period of just under a year most of them, at one point or another, were involved in some aspect of producing the new typesetter. The machine, which was sold in quantity for the first time in 1962, was called Linasec. It sold for a fraction of the cost of competing computerized typesetters. For each Linasec machine it built, Wang Labs was paid about thirty thousand dollars by Compugraphic.

Over the next three years Dr. Wang's corporation earned more than two million dollars from the construction of Linasecs alone. In fiscal year 1964 (which was actually the period from July 1, 1963 to the end of June 1964) total sales for Wang Laboratories passed the one-million-dollar mark for the first time. It seemed like a lot of money to Dr. Wang and his fellow workers, but it was really just pocket change compared with what was to come for the company in the years ahead. In the meantime, however, a serious setback occurred.

"The future looked very promising," Dr. Wang wrote about the Linasec's good fortunes. "But before I had time to really savor this success, I received a startling piece of news from Compugraphic: they had decided to manufacture Linasec themselves. Even though Wang Laboratories owned the patent on Linasec, Compugraphic had retained the right to manufacture the machines without paying a royalty. Because we had developed the machine under contract to Compugraphic, we had never attempted to market the machine under the Wang logo. At this point, we didn't have the people to market Linasec anyway. Thus we were helpless to do anything about the Compugraphic decision."[1]

Dr. Wang may have felt helpless in his business dealings with Compugraphic, but he was hardly powerless in general. In the decades to come, the experience with Linasec would be particularly helpful as Wang Labs developed its famous word-processing computers. But Dr. Wang had a more immediate solution to the problem of lost typesetter sales. At about the time Compugraphic made its decision, An was already at work developing a revolutionary electronic calculator.

The new invention came at a critical time. In 1964 Dr. Wang purchased eighty acres of land in the town of Tewksbury, Massachusetts, another suburb of Boston. Many people thought that he was foolish to purchase so much land for his company. But he went ahead anyway, and had a new building constructed to house his growing company. It was a carefully calculated move.

Today, many stores sell tiny calculators, not much larger than a credit card, for as little as five or ten dollars. In the mid-1960s, however, simple electronic calculators did not exist. Instead, most stores and offices used adding machines, large devices that used metal gears and other mechanical parts to add and subtract numbers. The gears were turned either by electric motors or by a large handle pulled by a human operator. Adding or subtracting numbers on these machines was nearly as simple as on a modern electronic calculator. Multiplication and division, however, was much more difficult, and even impossible on some models.

Large computers seemed to be able to multiply and divide, but they actually merely added and subtracted very quickly. To multiply 100 by 100, for example, a computer merely added 100 and 100, added 100 to the total, and repeated the process ninety-eight more times. Computers were already so fast that the time required to compute a series of one hundred addition operations—or even thousands—was hardly noticeable.

By the time Dr. Wang began designing his first electronic calculator, there were a few machines on the market that could perform calculations using electronic logic circuits. Such machines, however, generally required great mathematical skill to operate, or performed operations like multiplication and division in the same cumbersome way they were accomplished on true computers.

For centuries, mathematicians had known that numbers could be multiplied by adding their logarithms and divided by subtracting their logarithms. Logarithms were discovered in the sixteenth century by a Scottish nobleman named John Napier. Based on this discovery, he invented a simple machine, usually made of wood or ivory and called "Napier's bones," that helped figure out simple multiplication problems.

To understand simple logarithms, it is necessary to do a little math. Consider this short formula in the familiar base ten number system:

$$10^3 = 1000$$

In this example the raised numeral three, called an *exponent*, indicates that the number ten is being raised to the third power. A number raised to the first power always equals itself. In other words, $10^1 = 10$. A number raised to the second power, or *squared*, is equal to the number multiplied by itself: $10^2 = 10$ times 10, or 100. A number raised to the third power, or *cubed*, is equal to the product of the number multiplied by itself and then multiplied by itself again.

$10^1 = 10$

$10^2 = 10$ times 10, or, more simply, 100

$10^3 = 10$ times 10 times 10, or 1000

In the last example above, the exponent (the raised numeral three) is the logarithm of the number one thousand to the base ten. It shows that the base number (ten) must be raised to the third power to equal one thousand.

John Napier discovered that two numbers could be multiplied by adding their logarithms. This can be demonstrated easily. Simple multiplication shows that 10 times 100 equals 1000. Simple logarithms can be used to perform the same calculation:

10^1 times $10^2 = 10^3$

Stated in another way, this same formula can be read, "The number ten raised to the first power (10) times the number ten raised to the second power (100) equals the number ten raised to the third power (1000)." Simply by adding the exponents 1 and 2, we multiplied a two-digit number by a three-digit number to get a four-digit number.

Napier also discovered that division could be accomplished by subtracting exponents. See if you can divide the number one thousand by one hundred by subtracting exponents. The answer is simple:

10^3 divided by $10^2 = 10^1$

Unfortunately, most logarithms are not simple whole numbers such as the ones shown above. Most logarithms are fractions usually stated as decimals. Simple addition and subtraction become more difficult when a logarithm such as 0.6931471 is involved! The principle, nevertheless, is the same.

Dr. An Wang knew that many mathematical problems, including multiplication and division, could be performed on a relatively small electronic calculator if logarithms could be stored in the machine's memory. But to store a logarithm, even for just whole numbers between, say, one and a hundred million, would require a huge amount of memory. Not even the largest computers of the day had that much core memory.

At around the time Compugraphic decided to manufacture its own typesetters, An found a solution. It involved a formula that enabled an electronic circuit to figure out most logarithms for itself. To make this possible, Dr. Wang divided a great many different numbers into building blocks that mathematicians call factors. By storing logarithms for a relatively small number of *factors*, the machine could calculate logarithms for many numbers. The amount of memory needed was not excessive. He called his system the *factor-combining* method of determining logarithms.

With this breakthrough Wang Labs began marketing a revolutionary new calculator in early 1965. It was called LOCI, which stood for "logarithmic calculating instrument." Less than four years later An was awarded a U.S. patent for the LOCI circuit that performed the basic calculations. In the meantime Wang Laboratories began growing at a pace that soon left its competing calculator manufacturers in the dust.

At the time LOCI was introduced, a few other pioneering U.S. manufacturers also were making calculators that could fit on a desktop. Among the companies were Monroe, Olivetti, and Victor Comptometer. None of these machines, however, made use of the sophisticated approach of LOCI.

"To my knowledge," Dr. Wang wrote, "Wang Laboratories was the only company that discovered how to use the factor-combining method to generate logarithms. Ed Lesnick, an engineer who came to Wang Laboratories in 1968, says that when he was at Monroe, their chief programmer was still trying to figure out how Wang calculators generated logarithms."[2]

By 1966, sales from LOCIs averaged more than sixty-thousand dollars a month for Wang Labs. The little calculator was rapidly making up for the income lost by the Compugraphic decision. Even with brisk sales, however, LOCI was not the machine that sent the fortunes of Wang Labs into the stratosphere.

Despite its many innovations, LOCI had a number of problems. It was not as easy to use as modern calculators. To operate it, people had to have a basic understanding of logarithms and a few other concepts from the field of digital electronics. Because many fractions cannot be stated in terms of precise decimal numbers, the machine also made tiny mistakes, sometimes called "round-off errors," that could be quite noticeable. As Dr. Wang pointed out, LOCI "had the effect of producing an answer like 3.999999999 when you multiplied 2 x 2. While this answer might only be off by a factor of one in one billion, ordinary people feel more comfortable if they see the answer 4 when they multiply 2 x 2."3

Less than a year after the introduction of LOCI, Wang Laboratories began marketing another electronic calculator, called the Model 300. The new product included sophisticated circuits that corrected LOCI's problems. The Model 300 was nearly as easy to operate as today's electronic calculators. With little or no training, people with no knowledge of logarithms or digital electronics could solve long multiplication and division problems on it. At the same time, the new model had circuits to correct the round-off errors that sometimes looked so odd on LOCI.

The additional electronic circuits of the Model 300 took up much more space than LOCI. Dr. Wang and other engineers decided to separate the little keyboard and display from the rest of the circuits, which were housed in a box that could sit on the floor underneath a desk. Another circuit, called a *multiplexer*, was developed so that a number of people could use separate keyboards attached by cables to the same floor unit.

The Model 300 electronic calculator, introduced in late 1965, was a smashing success. For the first time, business people as well as scientists and engineers began buying Wang products. The company continued adding new calculators to its existing line. During the company's fiscal year from July 1, 1966, to June 30, 1967, total sales amounted to nearly seven million dollars. During the same period, the number of employees at Wang Labs increased dramatically, reaching more than four hundred in 1967.

The success of Wang calculators was helping Dr. Wang become even more financially secure. The timing was excellent. As the company's first calculators were being introduced, Juliette, An and Lorraine's third child and only daughter, was born. At the time, however, no one in the growing Wang family could have realized the years of even more explosive growth that lay ahead for Wang Laboratories.

At the Tewksbury office Dr. Wang managed to continue working as an engineer, even though more and more time had to be spent overseeing his growing number of employees. Many of the employees began calling him "the Doctor." Even as his company's fortunes began to soar, the Doctor continued to manage his business affairs quietly. At times he appeared almost shy. When he spoke, it was usually quietly, with a minimal number of well-chosen words. Despite it all, he clearly understood that his engineering skills were valuable ones. One coworker called him "a humble egomaniac."[4]

"When Dr. Wang must bawl you out," another employee from the era said, "it's more like being reproached by a sorrowful father than an angry boss."[5] Fortunately, he seldom had to scold the people he recruited to work for him.

With the success of the calculators, the Doctor began hiring people to work at Wang Laboratories who added enormously to the company's success over the next two decades. As one executive from the company put it, "The Doctor could pick winners."6

In Tewksbury, and later at the company's new headquarters in Lowell, Dr. Wang always had an office near his company's engineering department. He felt closest to those who developed new products for Wang Labs. Although the Doctor was a soft-spoken man himself, the process of developing new products was often a noisy one.

During research and development meetings Dr. Wang would quietly puff on a pipe as his engineers argued—often screamed—about the best way to design a new product. "He would let people call each other stupid and gang up on one another,"7 one high-ranking executive remembered.

Not all product decisions were technical ones. Philip Gaber, who at the time was managing Wang sales in the southern United States, recalled a telephone conversation he once had with the Doctor. "I told him we could sell a new calculator line better if it was orange, because I was trying to sell to the University of Tennessee, and it was a school color."8 Before long Wang Laboratories was producing a line of orange calculators.

In 1967 Dr. Wang decided to turn his company from a private corporation to a public one. By going public Wang Laboratories would be able to sell stock in a public market such as the huge New York Stock Exchange. People who bought the stock would become part owners of Wang Laboratories. The Doctor felt that he needed to raise money for his company. Although more and more calculators were being sold each year, Wang Labs had taken a number of bank loans to pay for the development and manufacturing costs of the various calculator models.

Because a public corporation sells its stock to people from all walks of life, its stock activities are carefully watched by the federal government and by state governments as well. To become a public corporation, Wang Laboratories had to file paperwork with the U.S. Securities and Exchange Commission (SEC) in Washington, D.C., as well as with government agencies in every state. It was not an easy task. SEC approval was delayed because officials did not understand the products that Wang Laboratories made. Two Wang employees had to travel to Washington to demonstrate one of the company's electronic calculators.

Dr. Wang and his financial advisors carefully planned how to make the corporation's first public stock offer. After much study it was decided to put up for sale 200,000 shares of stock at $12.50 per share. If the company could sell all that stock, it would raise $2.5 million. At the same time, Dr. Wang and his family would keep enough stock so that they still owned 65 percent of the company.

A telegram from the SEC advising Wang Laboratories that

it could begin publicly selling stock was received on August 23, 1967. Wang Laboratories' stock began selling the same day. The results were so stunning that they attracted nationwide attention.

In a story about hot new stocks, *Newsweek* magazine reported: "The most flabbergasting of the recent entries, however, is Wang Laboratories, Inc., which took only two days to soar from its offering price of $12.50 to $40, and closed last week at $43.75."9

Many people who worked along New York's Wall Street, the center of stock market activity in the United States, already used Wang calculators. They believed that Wang stock was worth much more than the original offering price. People were stampeding to buy it!

Many Wang employees had purchased stock shortly before it was offered to the general public. Most paid just $4.17 a share. Overnight, they saw the value of their stock grow by more than 1,000 percent. Dr. Wang wrote, "Wang shareholders, including myself, watched our personal fortunes increase in lockstep with the stock. There was jubilation in the offices. I remember hearing my secretary, who had exercised an option to buy a hundred shares, shout, 'I'm rich, I'm rich.'"10 Richest of all were Dr. Wang and his family.

According to the selling price established by traders on the New York Stock Exchange, Wang's 65 percent share of his company was worth about fifty million dollars. In a few more months, when the value of Wang stock rose as high as $120 per share, it was worth nearly three times as much.

Chapter 7

NEW DIRECTIONS

By the late 1960s, Wang Laboratories was the largest maker of electronic calculators in the United States. Its success put An Wang on his way to becoming one of the richest persons in America. But he seemed unwilling to take full advantage of his growing wealth.

At a time when he could have purchased a major department store with cash, he owned only two suits. He didn't enjoy traveling very much and preferred to relax with his family in his Lincoln home. Although he resisted all pressure to move to a more luxurious house, over the years he did make a few improvements. A tennis court was built; a swimming pool and a satellite television dish were added; a garage was transformed into a guardhouse. Eventually, he and Lorraine purchased a summer home in the seacoast town of Woods Hole, Massachusetts, as well as an oceanfront apartment in downtown Boston. In the late 1970s, he finally bowed to pressure from his staff and allowed a chauffeur to drive him to and from work each day.

"The Chinese tend to play a low-key role," Lorraine told a reporter from the *Boston Globe* newspaper. "They feel that if they keep silent and work hard, they'll be promoted."[1] Still, for both Lorraine and her husband, life as wealthy Americans must have been rewarding. Both had felt the sting of prejudice. An recalled a time, shortly after he and Lorraine were married, when a landlord refused to rent a vacant apartment to them, probably because of their Asian heritage.

Throughout his working life, Dr. Wang seemed to enjoy his work as an engineer and an inventor more than his increasingly important role as a business leader. Although he received little formal training in business, his instincts were keen. Perhaps his greatest skill, according to those who worked with him, was his sense of timing.

David Moros, one of Dr. Wang's chief engineers, said, "He made four or five major changes in direction over the years. He would say: here is my technology, here is where the big markets are going to be in the next round, and here is how I will play in them."[2] In the rapidly changing world of digital electronics, timing was a critical talent. But Dr. Wang's decision about his company's role as a producer of electronic calculators stunned nearly everyone around him.

In the late 1960s, at a time when Wang Laboratories was making a fortune designing and selling calculators, the Doctor decided to remove his company from that field entirely. It would take some time, he knew. But he also understood that his company would only continue to grow if it began to make new types of products. He was convinced, and was soon proved correct, that high profits from the manufacture of electronic calculators would soon all but vanish. Engineers and research scientists were already beginning to develop miniature electronic devices called *integrated circuits* that would make even complex calculators extremely cheap and easy to manufacture. It was time to find new products, and Dr. Wang began thinking about full-fledged computers.

In many respects, the most sophisticated Wang calculators from around 1970 were much like small computers. They had core memories. Programs could be written for them to partially automate repetitive calculating tasks. They had small tube displays, but they could also print out information on electric typewriters.

"We may talk about computers with technical people," Dr. Wang said in 1971, "but never with market men."3 Even though his advanced calculators were much like computers, the Doctor knew that his company, at least until now, was not prepared to enter the full-scale computer marketplace. Nevertheless, he also knew that his top-of-the-line calculators were close enough to true computers that his company might consider entering the computer business.

He felt that the demand for true computers was about to increase dramatically. A few years earlier, in 1964, two Dartmouth professors named John Kemeny and Tom Kurtz completed the development of a new computer language called BASIC (Beginner's All-Purpose Symbolic Instruction Code). For the first time, BASIC allowed people with little experience to write computer programs that were capable of solving relatively sophisticated problems.

Wang Labs attempted to make full-fledged computers beginning in 1967 and 1968. The earliest models, built around the central processing units of Wang calculators, suffered from a number of problems. The first machine, called the Model 4000, was completed in early 1968. As soon as Dr. Wang began using it, he knew it simply was not fast or versatile enough to compete with machines from manufacturers such as IBM and Digital Equipment Corporation (DEC), another Massachusetts electronics firm.

At the time DEC was making a name for itself by developing a new class of computers, called *minicomputers*. As opposed to larger machines, called *mainframes*, made by IBM and a few other manufacturers, minicomputers made very efficient use of relatively small amounts of core memory. While smaller and less expensive than mainframes, minis could perform valuable functions.

In late 1968 the Doctor led two teams working to develop two different minicomputers for Wang Labs. One machine, called the 3300 BASIC, was a promising effort but suffered a fatal flaw. Designed to work best with the easy-to-use BASIC programming language, the 3300 had to be made ready for BASIC by feeding it a binary program coded as holes punched into paper tape.

"The means chosen to load BASIC into the computer was

paper tape," Dr. Wang wrote. "The problem was that paper tape loads at the rate of ten bytes per second (which is extremely slow), and BASIC is a long program. Getting the 3300 going involved feeding huge ribbons of paper tape into the machine at a very slow rate. It took roughly forty minutes to load the program, and if something went wrong, you had to start the whole process over again."4

The other computer developed at the same time, the Model 700, seemed to show more promise. During its development, however, the Hewlett-Packard company announced, and soon began selling, a remarkable new calculator that threatened the market dominance of the best calculators produced by Wang Labs. Hewlett-Packard's 9100 series of calculators included small CRT screens that could display several lines of calculations. The machines could be programmed directly on a keyboard and also used magnetic cards to run prewritten programs that paused for operator input.

Dr. Wang was anxious to move away from the field, but he understood that electronic calculators still accounted for about 70 percent of his company's sales. He made the decision, therefore, to change the Model 700 from a minicomputer to a top-of-the-line electronic calculator, able to compete with the new challenge from Hewlett-Packard. For a time, it would enable his company to maintain its position as the nation's leading calculator maker. But he had little doubt that the need for new types of products was becoming more and more urgent.

The Model 700 was notable in several respects. Wang engineers were anxious to find a medium capable of storing more programs than the magnetic cards used by the Hewlett-Packard calculator. They soon discovered that digital information could be recorded on ordinary cassette tapes, at the time used only for music and voice recordings. Although they were eventually replaced by floppy disks, over the years a great many other companies also produced computers and other digital electronic devices that could read information stored on cassette tapes. The Model 700 was Wang Labs' last calculator to make use of Dr. Wang's Harvard invention, the memory cores. For most manufacturers, the era of ferrite core memories was about to end.

In 1970 California's Intel corporation began selling a tiny device, about the size of a fingernail, that could store two thousand bits of digital information and had other circuitry built into it as well. Somewhat optimistically, Intel officials called it a "computer on a chip." Other components were needed to help the chip act as a true computer, but it was clear that the age of the integrated circuit had arrived.

The integrated circuit, Intel's so-called computer chip, dramatically changed the scope and economics of the digital electronics industry. Over the next few years ROM and RAM memory chips rapidly replaced the computer memory cores Dr. Wang had invented at Harvard. More important to his present business, the Doctor knew that it would soon be possible to market full-featured calculators, like Wang's Model 3000 (which originally sold for $1,695) for far less. It would take some time, to be sure, but time is what the Doctor needed to find new products and new markets for his company.

In the meantime Wang Laboratories became the first company to purchase Intel's chips in quantity. They were used in a new series of business calculators. Still, the Doctor knew that computers, not calculators, had to form the backbone of his product line if his company was going to continue to grow.

In late 1972, Wang Labs began selling a new computer, the 2200, that solved the problems of earlier models. Instead of using paper tape to input preprogrammed information, the 2200 used cassette tapes, which were soon changed to floppy disks. Disks were preferable to tapes because information could be found on them more rapidly. The 2200 also used a CRT to display information. Its major innovation, however, was that it stored the BASIC language program in ROM chips developed by Intel. Since BASIC did not have to be loaded from paper or magnetic tapes, the 2200 computer was ready to work almost as soon as the power was turned on. Although it was gradually replaced by more powerful computers, the 2200 was sold for more than fifteen years. Even before the new computer was released, however, the Doctor began leading his company in a new direction that eventually led to a stunning success.

In November 1971, Dr. Wang held a press conference in New

York City. He announced that Wang was about to market a computerized typewriter. At the time, the automated typing field was dominated by IBM, which controlled about 80 percent of the market. During the conference, Dr. Wang was asked, "How do you think IBM will respond to your product?"

"There are two IBM vice-presidents in the back of the room," Dr. Wang replied. "Why don't you ask them?"[5] He also added that he didn't think IBM would feel threatened by his company. "Let's face it," he said, "computerized typewriters are just a sideline with IBM—we'll be tackling their little finger, not their right arm."[6] Although he didn't know it at the time, however, IBM was taking the challenge very seriously.

In the early 1970s companies such as IBM—and soon Wang and Xerox—were marketing computerized typewriters that were the forerunners of modern word-processing systems. By contemporary standards these machines were very primitive. None of them had a CRT to display information that was being entered. Instead, operators looked at words as they were being typed on paper. The principal advantage of the machines was that keystrokes were stored temporarily in RAM memory. An entire letter could be transferred for permanent storage to magnetic tape or, a bit later, to a floppy disk. If part of a letter needed to be changed, the typist could have the computer retype all the material that didn't need to be altered, stopping at lines where edits were necessary and typing in the new information.

The computerized typewriter, called the Model 1200, that Dr. Wang announced at the New York press conference was based on one of his own company's electronic calculators. That calculator used an IBM Selectric typewriter to print information. To change the calculator to a computerized typewriter, it was only necessary to change the operating system coded in its ROM. However, the fact that it used an IBM machine to type characters on paper soon caused problems.

In the early 1970s, many people considered the IBM Selectric to be the finest typewriter in the world. Offices everywhere used it as a stand-alone typewriter. IBM itself, as well as other companies such as Wang Labs, also found ways to attach it to computers to make primitive word-processing systems. It was highly reliable.

Because of the machine's good reputation, Wang executives were surprised to find that most of the Selectrics attached to their Model 1200 computer seemed to work poorly. Characters printed on paper were ragged and uneven. Many office workers who rented the system began to complain. At one point, the Doctor recalled, about 80 percent of the people using the Model 1200 canceled their orders. Because of these problems, Wang Labs suffered its first quarterly loss in history, during a three-month period in the summer of 1972. One of the people puzzled by the problem was a Wang executive named Ed Lesnick.

"Finally," Dr. Wang wrote, "Ed Lesnick called in a couple of

IBM servicemen to look at the Selectric. They immediately noticed that a part called a carriage stabilizing spring was missing. They put one in, and the machine worked. They also told us that all the machines IBM produced for their own markets had this spring. A survey of other machines revealed that the spring was missing in every machine we had."7

IBM officials insisted they had done nothing wrong and agreed to replace the missing parts in all Selectric typewriters purchased by Wang Laboratories. But real damage had been done. Off to such a poor start, sales of its first computerized typewriter never took off for Wang Labs. For several years, company profits were on a roller coaster ride, rising and falling with changes in the economy and always endangered by the constantly falling prices of electronic calculators, still one of the company's main product lines.

During this turbulent era, Frederick Wang, An and Lorraine's oldest child, began working for his father's company. It was an old Chinese custom that a father's first son would eventually take over the family business. Although he was a skilled computer programmer, young Frederick hardly started at the top, beginning part-time work while still a college student at Brown University. Some of his earliest duties involved low-level programming chores.

In one task, however, it was clear that he was being groomed for bigger things. Early in his career at his father's company, he was given the assignment of creating an organizational chart for Wang Labs. This type of chart usually consists of boxes and lines showing which bosses are responsible for which employees. Fred's finished chart showed 136 people reporting directly to An Wang.

There was little doubt about who was in charge at Wang Labs.

An Wang sits in front of one of his Wang Word Processors

Chapter 8

THE WORD IS WANG!

In 1975 the Xerox corporation released a new computerized typing system that included its Diablo printer. Although it was slow by today's standards, the Diablo was capable of printing twice as fast as the computerized systems developed by Wang and IBM for the Selectric typewriter. Although the Xerox system did not include a CRT, its sheer speed made it more than competitive.

At the same time a few small companies, including AES and Vydec, began marketing word-processing systems that did include a CRT display for editing. The programs that ran the systems, however, were far from easy to use and sales were never great. Dr. Wang decided it was time to develop a new system from the ground up.

An engineer named Harold Koplow, who had joined the company in 1968, was put in charge of the development team. His principal assistant was another engineer named David Moros. Koplow and Moros began their work in a very unusual way. Instead of designing a machine, they wrote a book of instructions first. Several editions of the instructions were passed around to company executives and secretaries who suggested ways to do things more simply. Only when the operating manual was finished would work on the actual product begin.

Not everyone was satisfied with the manual. Some salesmen complained that it would hurt sales of the existing computerized typewriter. Some technical people insisted that in making it easy to use, the new system lacked needed features. "They said it would never fly," Harold Koplow remembered.

"I don't care what they say," Dr. Wang answered. "I like it. You build it."[1] As always, the Doctor's decision was the one that mattered at Wang Labs. Work on the company's new word-processing system began at once.

"The new machine would be CRT-based rather than typewriter-based," Dr. Wang wrote. "This meant that the user could manipulate text by moving words as they appeared on the screen. . . . The most striking difference between this new system and the other CRT-based word processing systems already on the market was that it would be driven by a series of menus designed to guide the user through its operations. At every decision point, the secretary would be presented with a clear set of choices, written in a language anyone could understand. Getting the word processor to do what she wanted would be a simple matter of responding to these choices. The machine we envisioned would without doubt be the most user-friendly machine on the market at that time. It was perhaps the first computer with which an ordinary person could interact."[2]

During the closing months of 1975 and the early part of 1976, work on the new machine proceeded rapidly. It was named the WPS, which stood for Word Processing System. Near the end of the development cycle, Wang engineers ran into a snag. They had difficulty making the final connections between the small computer and the CRT and typewriter terminals. The Doctor himself designed the final link.

In charge of marketing the new system was a sales executive named Carl Masi. Months before the WPS was first sold, Masi knew that he would have little trouble marketing it. Everyone who used the new machine immediately fell in love with it. "They took one look at the screen and saw the magic we could do with words,"3 Masi remembered. At the time, an overwhelming majority of people had never seen a CRT-based word processor. There certainly had never been one as easy to operate as the Wang WPS.

Dr. Wang decided to introduce the WPS at a New York City trade show, called Syntopican, to be held in June 1976. Work to finalize a test model suitable for demonstrating at the show rushed ahead.

While all this was going on, Dr. Wang faced another problem. In three of the past four years, sales of Wang products had not been as high as expected. Preparing to release a revolutionary new product, the Doctor knew that he had to raise money to pay for final development and the enormous manufacturing and marketing expenses that went with it.

Many public corporations raise money by issuing new stock certificates. Dr. Wang was reluctant to do so. Over the years, the amount of stock owned by him and his immediate family had fallen to 52 percent of the total stock in the company. If it fell to 50 percent or less, he could lose control of his own corporation. The Doctor and his top advisors studied this problem as they watched over the final development of the new word-processing system.

In June 1976 three Wang Labs salespeople introduced the WPS at the Syntopican show in New York City. In a rush of overtime and hard work, Wang engineers had the computer, program, keyboard, and CRT monitor working together perfectly. But they were unable to get the printer up and running in time for the show. It hardly mattered. The WPS made a stunning debut.

"We had a small booth on the main floor of the convention hall as well as a hospitality suite at the Hilton," the Doctor wrote, "where the show was held. Word spread like wildfire about the machine, and within moments of the first demonstration, people were lined up ten deep at the booth. The hospitality suite became so jammed that we had to issue invitations in order to control the crowds. . . .

"The three demonstrators were absolutely exhausted by the end of the first day," Dr. Wang continued, "so that night Carl Masi had them train the entire New York sales force to give demonstrations. That it was possible to do this proved that the system was incredibly easy to use."4

A few days later, when the convention ended, everyone associated with Wang Laboratories knew that the company had a major hit within its grasp. Dr. Wang put his son Frederick in charge of a separate sales force to market the new word processor. He then put additional energy into finding money to support the rapidly growing manufacturing costs the company was about to face.

After a series of meetings, the Doctor and his financial advisors decided that issuing stock would be the best way to raise the money needed to support the hot machine. His inner circle included John Cunningham, a vice president at the time and later the president of Wang Labs; Harry Chou, treasurer; and Ed Grayson, corporate secretary. To keep control of his company, Dr. Wang would have to severely limit the voting power people who bought the new stock could have in the affairs of his company. By controlling 52 percent of the vote Dr. Wang himself now controlled every aspect of his company's decisions, but only by the slim margin of 2 percent. He wanted to keep it that way.

The New York Stock Exchange has complex rules regulating the stock corporations can sell in its marketplace. Dr. Wang and his advisors wanted to list a new class of stock that had just one-tenth the voting power of previous Wang stock. By doing that, the Doctor would be able to maintain control of his company while at the same time raising needed cash.

Unfortunately, officials at the New York Stock Exchange decided that the complicated arrangement would violate its rules. Stung by the rejection of their plans, Dr. Wang and his advisors considered their options. They knew that the New York exchange was not the only game around. Other stock exchanges could be found in many American cities, including Philadelphia, Chicago, Los Angeles, and San Francisco. There was even another exchange in New York City, the American Stock Exchange.

Curiously, written rules regulating the type of stock Wang Labs was trying to offer were identical for both the New York and the American stock exchanges. But officials at the American Stock Exchange read them somewhat differently. They decided that it would be perfectly acceptable for Wang Labs to move to its exchange and offer exactly the kind of new stock Dr. Wang was interested in selling.

The stock, with limited voting rights, was called Class B. The old stock, with full voting rights, was called Class A. Both classes of Wang stock began selling on the American Stock Exchange on April 21, 1976. A few people wondered if the stock Dr. Wang was offering would turn out to be a good deal for investors. Almost exactly ten years later, Dr. Wang offered this answer: "Someone who bought a hundred shares of Class B stock on April 21, 1976, for an investment of $1,250 saw those hundred shares become two thousand shares worth $40,000 . . . ten years later."5

It may be hard to imagine what those figures mean. The compound interest rate, similar to what a bank gives people who set up savings accounts, amounted to more than 35 percent per year for Class B Wang stock. In the 1990s interest rates granted by banks averaged around 5 percent. People who bought Dr. Wang's stock and sold it ten years later made a very wise investment. On the other hand, investors who held that stock for five more years didn't fare nearly as well.

While tycoon Wang was floating in an ocean of high finance, demand for his new word-processing system was spreading like a fire on the prairie. Some Wang salesmen could hardly contain their enthusiasm. "We created a whole new job category, word processing,"[6] one of them claimed.

David Moros, one of the principal engineers on the project, recalled that even the early problems with the machine pointed to its acceptance in a growing number of offices. Static electricity, often generated by friction between carpets and clothing in dry weather, tended to damage delicate microchips inside the machine. "At the beginning," Moros said, "we would have to go in and remove the whole thing to fix it. Secretaries would scream and say, 'Don't take my machine away.'"[7]

The Doctor noted that until the arrival of his WPS, many typing duties tended to be inefficient and uninteresting for employees. "It was really all about trying to make office workers more productive so they would get more enjoyment out of their jobs,"[8] he said. This fun, of course, came with a price. A fully-loaded Wang WPS, complete with a fast hard disk drive, cost thirty thousand dollars.

The astounding success of the WPS certainly helped Dr. Wang enjoy his job. In 1976, the same year the new word processor was introduced, Dr. Wang went shopping for land to expand his corporate headquarters. He soon found it along Route 128 in Lowell, Massachusetts. The area would soon become the center of high-tech activity in New England.

In Lowell, Wang Laboratories purchased a building constructed in the 1950s by CBS Electronics. Sixteen additional acres were included in the purchase. The land would give the company room to expand, if that was necessary. In the beginning Wang executives considered renting out half of the building. The Doctor decided to wait. Before a year was up, the building was filled to capacity with Wang products and busy Wang employees. Before a decade had passed, new buildings had to be constructed, amounting to almost ten times the total area of the original building.

Wang word-processing systems just sold and sold and sold. In 1976, the year the WPS was introduced, Wang Labs was not even included in *Datamation* magazine's list of the top fifty American computer manufacturers. By the following year, it was number thirty-two. Two years later, it was number twenty-five. By 1981, it had climbed to 11th place. Sales skyrocketed from less than $100 million in 1976 to $1.1 billion in 1982. By the early 1980s, Wang Laboratories owned more than one-third of the worldwide market for word-processing machines.

Late in 1979 fifty-nine-year-old Dr. An Wang took time to gloat a bit, especially when he thought about his old business rival IBM. "You know," he said, "IBM was 1,000 times bigger than us ten years ago. This year they will be only 50 times bigger. Exponentially, we're gaining on them."9 For the next few years, Wang Labs would get a little closer in its efforts to overtake the industry giant. Depending on which expert you listen to, for a few years they may well have taken the word-processing crown away from the long-time champion.

Above: Dr. An and Lorraine Wang applaud other inductees during Wang's induction into the National Inventors Hall of Fame in 1988. Below: Dr. Wang, his wife Lorraine, and his sons Fred and Courtney attended a dedication ceremony at Boston Massachusetts General Hospital's ambulatory-care building in 1985.

Chapter 9

THE EMPIRE STRIKES BACK

There is one thing that the heads of all the computer companies in the world—no matter how large or small—have in common. We have to deal with IBM, either as the company that already dominates our market, or as the Goliath that might at any moment enter it. It is not a prospect that any CEO [Chief Executive Officer] takes lightly.[1]

— Dr. An Wang, 1986

In 1982 International Business Machines introduced its famous PC, or Personal Computer. In doing so IBM joined a growing list of smaller companies selling a class of machines called microcomputers. Companies who beat IBM to the market with microcomputers included Apple, Commodore, Atari, and Tandy. Although many of the earlier microcomputers were fascinating machines capable of some serious work, most business people regarded them as expensive toys. Often called "home computers," most were considered suitable presents for children.

The IBM microcomputer, however, took the working world by storm. In some respects early IBM PCs were not very good machines. The PC's central processing unit was more advanced than the so-called home computers, but it suffered from a number of problems. One was what many engineers considered to be a design flaw. In every byte of information it processed the machine wasted a precious data bit for unnecessary error detection. Because part of its operating system was often stored on a floppy disk, the IBM PC sometimes squeezed less information onto a floppy than the "toy" computers available at a fraction of its cost. Some models were equipped with an expensive hard disk drive that broke down alarmingly soon.

One thing about the PC was undeniable, however. It was produced by IBM, and that was a name nearly every person in business recognized and trusted. They knew that IBM had the economic power and the technical know-how to fix just about any problem imaginable. And that is just what the company did. In two short years, IBM introduced the XT and then the vastly improved AT, or "Advanced Technology," microcomputer. With the AT, IBM produced a computer capable of truly enormous amounts of high-speed work.

As it developed and released its new computers, IBM did one other remarkable thing. It was an act that many IBM executives probably regret today. The company published full specifications for each machine, explaining in great detail how it worked; how machine language programs could be written for it; and even gave enough information so that other companies could design hardware to fit inside its steel cabinet. Nearly overnight a huge industry of small, high-tech companies began preparing programs and hardware products for the IBM PC. With so much competition prices were driven down. Soon companies began selling inexpensive "IBM clones," complete computers that (usually) worked just like the IBM models but sometimes cost far less to buy.

In this way IBM microcomputers and their look-alike clones conquered the business world. Personal computers began showing up on nearly every office worker's desk. Many were made by IBM. Some were made by other manufacturers, but most followed the engineering guidelines established by IBM. A few people argued that this was not the only way to go. They pointed to products such as Apple's Macintosh computer and a few advanced products announced by Wang Labs as proof that there were other, perhaps superior, basic designs. But the battle was really over before it began.

As good as it was, the Wang word processing system was dedicated to one task only. Microcomputers from IBM and other manufacturers could perform well as word processors and do many other things as well. They could, for example, keep financial records or other statistics in highly flexible formats called *spreadsheets*. They could be used to maintain databases of all sorts of information that could be reorganized and displayed in ways a word processor simply could not handle. They could even be used to play the latest video arcade games.

At the start of the 1980s Dr. Wang was sixty years old. A few years later, around 1982, he began spending a bit less of his time in the office. The following year he formally retired as the president of the company he had founded, although he continued to serve as chairman of the board. He named John Cunningham, a Wang employee since 1967, as the company's new president.

In 1983, the same year Dr. Wang retired and a year before IBM released its AT computer, some industry experts predicted that Wang Labs soon would be in trouble. "It is not clear that Wang is in the mainstream of the office anymore," one said. "The perception is that Wang's product is a little tired and expensive,"2 said another. Still, Wang Labs was hardly out of the battle. Its revenues for fiscal 1983 amounted to $1.5 billion, up 33 percent from the year before.

On October 4, 1983, the company announced a total of fourteen new products in the hope of drawing attention away from the IBM juggernaut. A spokesman promised that delivery of the new machines would begin by the following May. The most remarkable new device was called the Professional Image Computer. It included a special camera capable of sending photographic images to the computer for digital storage. The images could then be attached to print documents or even sent to other computers. On the same day Wang also announced a number of products that could work with IBM computers. As early as 1983 Wang executives realized that they would now have to learn to coexist with IBM in the office.

The new products were plagued by problems. The Professional Image Computer, promised by May 1984, did not begin shipping until early 1985. A year later, only three hundred units had been sold. In 1985 the Doctor was forced to return to daily operations in the Lowell headquarters. A major office automation project, called Wang Office, had been shipped to purchasers filled with errors. Dr. Wang led a team in efforts to debug it. In the meantime, sales of IBM computers continued to grow.

Remarkably, just at the time his company was beginning its decline, Dr. Wang was recognized as the fifth-richest man in America. According to *Forbes* magazine, his personal wealth in 1984 amounted to $1.6 billion. The *Boston Globe* soon noted that he was the richest person in New England. But despite his great personal wealth, much of it tied up in Wang Laboratories stock, the Doctor no longer had the youthful energy he needed to turn around his ailing company.

In July 1985 John Cunningham, at the time the only man besides the Doctor to serve as president of Wang Labs, announced that he was quitting to take a lesser paying job. At about the same time, the company announced that it had lost $109 million during the latest three-month period. It was the company's first quarterly loss in more than twenty years.

In 1986 An and Lorraine's son Frederick became the newest president of the troubled company. By then, however, there seemed to be little anyone could do to solve the firm's problems. On August 7, 1989, three weeks after Boston doctors operated on his father for throat cancer, Fred Wang resigned. Just two weeks earlier, the company had announced a $424 million loss for the one-year period ending June 30. Because the company was no longer considered financially strong enough to guarantee the bank loans it had received, bankers swarmed all over the company headquarters, approving or disapproving every important move.

Perhaps it was Dr. An Wang's training in the teachings of Confucius that helped him maintain a sense of balance during his final years on the board of his troubled company. By the time you read this the company he founded may no longer exist. It will certainly be a different place than it was when it revolutionized the working world with a new generation of electronic calculators, and then did it again with the first generation of modern word processors.

Time cannot take away Dr. Wang's enormous accomplishments. In the final decade of his life, he contributed huge sums of money to worthy causes. He donated four million dollars to save downtown Boston's Performing Arts Center, which was soon renamed the Wang Center for Performing Arts. He gave gifts amounting to four million dollars to Harvard University, and another million to neighboring Wellesley College, where Lorraine once studied.

He spent six million dollars creating the Wang Institute of

Graduate Studies in the state of Massachusetts near the New Hampshire border. There, the emphasis is on advanced study in software engineering and Chinese culture.

Perhaps his most important contribution of all was the construction of a fifteen-million-dollar factory in downtown Boston's Chinatown neighborhood. That factory provided jobs for as many as three hundred inner-city people.

"The theme of my philanthropy has been the same as my approach to technology: to find a need and fill it," he wrote. "I benefited from the Boston community in practical, material ways, and I feel obligated to repay the community in practical, material ways. When we enter society at birth, we receive an inheritance from the people who lived before us. It is our responsibility to augment that inheritance for those who succeed us. I feel that all of us owe the world more than we received when we were born."3

NOTES

Chapter 1

1. Lawrence Edelman, "Wang Loses $48.9 Million in Quarter—Analysts: Firm Still Hasn't Hit Bottom," *Boston Globe* (April 25, 1991).

2. Dennis Hevesi, "An Wang, 70, Is Dead of Cancer; Inventor and Maker of Computers," *The New York Times* (March 25, 1990).

3. Ibid.

4. Ronald Rosenberg, "IBM Partnership Wins Praise From Fred Wang," *Boston Globe* (June 20, 1991).

Chapter 2

1. Dr. An Wang (with Eugene Linden), *Lessons* (Reading, Mass.: Addison-Wesley Publishing Company, Inc., 1986), 11.

2. Ibid., 13-14.

3. Ibid., 16.

4. Ibid., 17.

5. Nathan Cobb, "The Very Private An Wang," *Boston Globe* (October 2, 1983).

6. Wang, *Lessons*, 21-22.

7. Ibid., 22.

8. Ibid., 25.

9. Ibid., 27-28.

10. Ibid., 28-29.

Chapter 3

1. Dr. An Wang (with Eugene Linden), *Lessons* (Reading, Mass.: Addison-Wesley Publishing Company, Inc., 1986), 31.

2. Ibid., 36.

3. Ibid., 39.

4. Arthur M. Lewis, "Dr. Wang's Toughest Case," *Fortune* (February 3, 1986): 107.

5. Wang, *Lessons*, 53.

6. Ibid., 52.

7. Ibid., 56-57.

Chapter 4

1. Dr. An Wang (with Eugene Linden), *Lessons* (Reading, Mass.: Addison-Wesley Publishing Company, Inc., 1986), 71.

2. Nathan Cobb, "The Very Private An Wang," *Boston Globe* (October 2, 1983).

3. "The Guru of Gizmos," *Time* (November 17, 1980): 81.

4. Wang, *Lessons*, 81.

5. Ibid., 86.

6. Ibid., 87.

7. Nathan Cobb, "The Very Private An Wang," *Boston Globe* (October 2, 1983).

8. Wang, *Lessons*, 37.

9. "Wang Challenges Mighty IBM for a Market," *Business Week* (November 13, 1971): 104.

Chapter 5

1. Dr. An Wang (with Eugene Linden), *Lessons* (Reading, Mass.: Addison-Wesley Publishing Company, Inc., 1986), 100.

2. Ibid., 83.

3. Ibid., 111-112.

Chapter 6

1. Dr. An Wang (with Eugene Linden), *Lessons* (Reading, Mass.: Addison-Wesley Publishing Company, Inc., 1986), 121.

2. Ibid., 127.

3. Ibid., 131.

4. Nathan Cobb, "The Very Private An Wang," *Boston Globe* (October 2, 1983).

5. "Wang Challenges Mighty IBM for a Market," *Business Week* (November 13, 1971): 104.

6. Charles Stein, "The Rise and Fall of a Computer Giant," *Boston Globe* (November 26, 1989).

7. Ibid.

8. "Wang Challenges Mighty IBM for a Market," *Business Week* (November 13, 1971): 104.

9. "Wang!" *Newsweek* (September 18, 1967): 81.

10. Wang, *Lessons*, 150.

Chapter 7

1. Nathan Cobb, "The Very Private An Wang," *Boston Globe* (October 2, 1983).

2. Charles Stein, "The Rise and Fall of a Computer Giant," *Boston Globe* (November 26, 1989).

3. "Wang Challenges Mighty IBM for a Market," *Business Week* (November 13, 1971): 106.

4. Dr. An Wang (with Eugene Linden), *Lessons* (Reading, Mass.: Addison-Wesley Publishing Company, Inc., 1986), 164–165.

5. Ibid., 174.

6. "Wang Challenges Mighty IBM for a Market," *Business Week* (November 13, 1971): 102.

7. Wang, *Lessons*, 176.

Chapter 8

1. Charles Stein, "The Rise and Fall of a Computer Giant," *Boston Globe* (November 26, 1989).

2. Dr. An Wang (with Eugene Linden), *Lessons* (Reading, Mass.: Addison-Wesley Publishing Company, Inc., 1986), 178.

3. Charles Stein, "The Rise and Fall of a Computer Giant," *Boston Globe* (November 26, 1989).

4. Wang, *Lessons*, 182–183.

5. Ibid., 196.

6. Charles Stein, "The Rise and Fall of a Computer Giant," *Boston Globe* (November 26, 1989).

7. Ibid.

8. Karen Berney, "An Wang: Getting to the Essentials," *Nation's Business* (December 1987): 85.

9. "The Doctor's Winning Formula," *Forbes* (January 7, 1980):170.

Chapter 9

1. Dr. An Wang (with Eugene Linden), *Lessons* (Reading, Mass.: Addison-Wesley Publishing Company, Inc., 1986), 91.

2. "The First Hint of Trouble at Wang," *Business Week* (October 17, 1983): 45.

3. Wang, *Lessons*, 237.

AN WANG 1920-1990

1920 An Wang is born in Shanghai, China, on February 7. The Panama Canal opens.
Robert Edwin Peary, discoverer of the North Pole, dies (born 1865). United States
passes Nineteenth Amendment, giving women the right to vote. The League of
Nations is established.

1921 First congress of the Chinese Communist party (CCP) is held. Albert Einstein wins
Nobel Prize in physics for discovering photoelectric effect.

1922 The former Union of Soviet Socialist Republics (U.S.S.R.) is established. Benito
Mussolini becomes dictator of Italy.

1923 Kuomintang (KMT) — the Nationalist party of China — splits into the left and the
right wings. Mustafa Kemal (Ataturk) establishes the Republic of Turkey. Nazi
party leader Adolf Hitler is imprisoned for an unsuccessful coup attempt.

1924 U.S. severely restricts immigration. The first Kuomintang national congress is held
at Canton.

1925 Hitler publishes volume one of *Mein Kampf.*

1926 The Wang family moves from Shanghai to Kun San. Germany is admitted to the
League of Nations. Kodak produces the first 16-mm movie film.

1927 Chiang Kai-shek purges and executes members of the Communist party. Charles A.
Lindbergh makes first solo airplane flight.

1928 The Nationalists, under Chiang Kai-shek, unite China under one government; national government moves to Nanking. Walt Disney releases first Mickey Mouse film. Alexander Fleming discovers penicillin.

1929 U.S. stock market crashes; Great Depression begins; worldwide economic crisis follows.

1930 Hitler's Nazi party gains a majority in German elections. Planet Pluto is discovered by C.W. Tombaugh of Lowell Observatory.

1931 Japan invades and occupies Manchuria and parts of Inner Mongolia.

1932 James Chadwick discovers the neutron. Franklin Delano Roosevelt wins landslide presidential victory.

1933 U.S. passes Twenty-first Amendment, repealing prohibition.

1934 The CCP, led by Mao Zedong, begins the epic Long March to Shensi Province.

1935 Mass student demonstration in China leads to the creation of an anti-Japanese leftist movement.

1936 An Wang's mother dies in Kun San. Chiang Kai-shek is kidnapped by his generals who forced him to declare war on Japan. Franklin Roosevelt is reelected president. Mussolini and Hitler proclaim the Roman-Berlin Axis.

1937 Nanking falls to the Japanese.

1938 Japanese take over city of Canton, China.

1939 Francisco Franco becomes dictator of Spain. Germany invades Poland; World War II begins (ends 1945). Igor Sikorsky constructs the first helicopter.

1940 An Wang graduates from college and starts teaching at Chiao Tung University (now spelled Jiao Tong University). France is occupied by Germany. Roosevelt is elected president for a third time. A puppet government is established in China.

1941 Germany invades the Soviet Union. Japanese bomb U.S. military base at Pearl Harbor; U.S. and Great Britain declare war on Japan.

1942 "Manhattan Project" of intensive atomic research begins in the U.S. Physicist Enrico Fermi splits the atom.

1943 General Chiang Kai-shek is elected president of the Chinese Republic.

1944 Mark I, the automatic sequence controlled calculator, is installed at Harvard University.

1945 An Wang leaves China for further studies in America; he starts post-graduate studies in applied physics at Harvard University. U.S. President Roosevelt dies and is succeeded by Vice-President Harry S Truman. The first atomic bomb is detonated near Alamogordo, New Mexico. U.S. drops first atomic bombs on Hiroshima and Nagasaki, Japan; Hitler commits suicide; Mussolini is killed; Germany and Japan surrender to the Allies; World War II ends. China regains control of Manchuria and Taiwan. The United Nations is established.

1946 An Wang goes to Ottawa, Canada, for a brief period. Two scientists from the University of Pennsylvania show that vacuum tubes can replace the electromechanical switches of the Mark I. The first electronic computer (ENIAC) is developed, containing 18,000 vacuum tubes. United States grants independence to the Philippines. Winston Churchill of Great Britain gives "Iron Curtain" speech. United Nations General Assembly holds its first session in London.

1947 India and Pakistan become independent. Scientists invent the transistor at the Bell Laboratories. U.S. Secretary of State George Marshall proposes the European Recovery Program, also called the Marshall Plan.

1948 Dr. An Wang earns a Ph.D. in applied physics and engineering; he is named a research fellow at the Harvard Computation Laboratory; he invents a magnetic core memory for computers; meets Lorraine Chiu, a student at Wellesley College.

1949 An Wang marries Lorraine; he files papers with the U.S. Patent Office for patenting core memory. The Electronic Discrete Sequential Automatic Computer (EDSAC) is completed at Cambridge University in England. The Chinese Communists win a total victory in China. People's Republic of China is proclaimed with Mao Zedong as its chairman and leader. Possession of firearms becomes illegal in China. Eleven Communists in the U.S. are convicted of conspiracy to overthrow the government.

1950 Frederick Wang, An and Lorraine Wang's first son, is born. Korean War begins. A thirty-year Chinese-Soviet Treaty is signed.

1951 Dr. Wang resigns from Harvard University and starts his own company, Wang Laboratories, with a total investment of $600. Wang Labs set up an exhibition booth at the Institute for Radio Engineering convention in Manhattan. The first Universal Automatic Computer (UNIVAC) — the first electronic computer for commercial purpose — is installed at the U.S. Census Bureau. U.S. Congress passes Twenty-second Amendment, setting two terms (eight years) as the maximum service for president. Color television is introduced in the U.S.

1952 Dr. Wang becomes a consultant to develop a specialized digital component. General Dwight D. Eisenhower is elected president and Richard M. Nixon becomes vice-president of the United States. King George VI of England dies; his daughter Elizabeth II, becomes Queen. The first hydrogen bomb is exploded at Eniwetok Atoll in the Pacific Ocean.

1953 Dr. Wang agrees to work part-time as a consultant for International Business Machines (IBM). Korean War ends; Korea is divided along 38th parallel into North and South Korea. China institutes its first five-year plan to promote industrialization. Joseph Stalin of the former U.S.S.R. dies. Nikita Khrushchev becomes head of Soviet Communist Party Central Committee.

1954 The first electronic computer in regular business use is installed in London at the Lyons Electronic Office (LEO). Communists in Vietnam take Dien Bien Phu and occupy Hanoi.

1955 Dr. Wang formally receives a patent for the invention of magnetic memory cores; Wang Laboratories becomes a corporation. Dr. and Lorraine Wang become U.S. citizens. China begins agricultural reforms by promoting collective method of agriculture. U.S. begins sending aid to Vietnam. Dictator Juan Perón of Argentina is overthrown.

1956 Dr. Wang sells his patent for core memories to IBM for one-half million dollars. Hungarians revolt against Soviet occupation of their country; Soviet troops invade Hungary. Israeli army invades Sinai Peninsula. Pakistan declares itself an Islamic country. Gamal Abdel Nasser becomes president of Egypt.

1957 Many Chinese dissidents are sent for reeducation in labor camps; the Chinese government seizes small family plots. Andrei Gromyko becomes Soviet foreign minister. Soviets launch first man-made satellites, *Sputnik I* and *II*, to circle the earth. European Common Market is established.

1958 Work force at the Wang Laboratories numbers ten. The first solid-state electronic computer is developed in Philadelphia; it has 100 times the capacity and 10 times the speed of the first electronic computer. China begins the Great Leap Forward (1958-60); emphasis is stressed on the development of labor-intensive industries.

U.S. launches its first satellite. Alaska becomes forty-ninth state of the U.S. Charles de Gaulle becomes president of the fifth republic of France. U.S. establishes National Aeronautics and Space Administration (NASA).

1959 Wang Laboratories reach an agreement with the Warner & Swasey Company of Cleveland for manufacturing Weditrol printed circuit boards. Among widespread violence and rebellion against Chinese rule, the Dalai Lama — the Tibetan spiritual leader — takes exile in India. Hawaii becomes fiftieth U.S. state. Fidel Castro overthrows Cuban dictator Fulgencio Batista and becomes president.

1960 The UNIVAC 1107 electronic computer employs Thin-Film memory; its operational speed is measured in billionths of a second (nanoseconds). The Soviet Union withdraws its technical help from China; Chinese government returns small family plots to people. Nixon and John F. Kennedy hold first televised debates between presidential candidates; Kennedy defeats Nixon in presidential election. Leonid Brezhnev becomes president of the U.S.S.R.

1961 The first mobile computer center is established by Remington Rand Univac. U.S. breaks diplomatic ties with Cuba. Berlin Wall is erected.

1962 Linasec, a typesetting machine developed by Compugraphics and the Wang Laboratories, is introduced in the market. A serious Cold War crisis is avoided when Soviet Union agrees to remove missiles from Cuba. U.S. establishes military advisors in South Vietnam.

1963 President Kennedy is assassinated in Dallas; Vice-President Lyndon B. Johnson becomes president of the United States. Reverend Martin Luther King, Jr. is arrested in protest marches in Birmingham, Alabama.

1964 Total sales for Wang Laboratories pass the one-million-dollar mark for the first time. Dr. Wang purchases 80 acres of land in Tewksbury, Massachusetts. Beginner's All-Purpose Symbolic Instruction Code (BASIC) language is developed. IBM produces the Magnetic Tape/Selectric Typewriter. China becomes the fifth nation to explode a nuclear bomb. Vietnam War escalates. Alexei Kosygin becomes prime minister and Leonid Brezhnev becomes Communist party secretary in the U.S.S.R. after Soviet dictator Khrushchev is toppled in a coup.

1965 Logarithmic calculating instrument (LOCI), a revolutionary new calculator is developed by Wang Laboratories. Model 300 electronic calculator is introduced. U.S.S.R. supplies arms to North Vietnam. Antiwar demonstrations sweep U.S. Great Britain celebrates 750th anniversary of the Magna Carta. Great Proletarian Cultural Revolution in China starts (finishes 1969).

1966 Sales from Wang Lab's LOCI calculators average more than $60,000 a month. All Chinese schools and universities are closed to allow students to participate in the Cultural Revolution; more and more students participate in the Red Guards groups. One million Red Guards assemble in huge rallies in Tiananmen Square. President Johnson of U.S. tours the Far East.

1967 Number of employees at the Wang Laboratories reaches four hundred; Wang Labs becomes a public corporation. Attempts to make full-fledged computers start at Wang Labs. Arab nations and Israel engage in Six-Day War; Israel defeats Arab nations. U.S. bombs Hanoi, North Vietnam. China detonates its first hydrogen bomb.

1968 The first computer — Model 4000 — is completed at the Wang Labs. Nixon is elected president. Soviet Union invades Czechoslovakia. Albania withdraws from the Warsaw Pact. The Reverend Martin Luther King, Jr. is assassinated in Memphis. *Apollo 8* of U.S. is the first spacecraft to orbit the moon.

1969 China declares the Soviet Union its principal enemy. Neil Armstrong of U.S. is the first man to walk on the moon. Ho Chi-Minh, president of the Democratic Republic of Vietnam, dies. China completes first successful underground nuclear test.

1970 First computer chip storing thousands of bits of digital information is introduced by California's Intel Corporation. After a coup in Cambodia, Prince Norodom Sihanouk establishes a government in exile in Beijing. China launches an earth-orbiting satellite. U.S. invades Cambodia. China establishes diplomatic relations with Canada and Italy. *Apollo 13* is launched from Cape Kennedy.

1971 Dr. Wang announces development of a computerized typewriter at a press conference in New York. Henry Kissinger, U.S. national security adviser, makes a secret trip to China. People's Republic of China is admitted to the United Nations; Taiwan loses its UN membership. American Ping-Pong team visits China. Chairman Mao invites President Nixon to China.

1972 Wang Labs start selling a computer called the 2200; Wang Labs suffer their first quarterly loss. President Nixon meets with Mao Zedong in Peking. Twenty countries (including Japan and West Germany) establish diplomatic relations with China. Nixon is reelected president; he is the first U.S. president to visit China and Moscow.

1973 U.S. and China exchange liaison offices. Cease-fire is declared in Vietnam. Middle East unrest causes oil prices to double, creating worldwide energy crisis.

1974 Nixon resigns as president because of the Watergate scandal. Charles A. Lindbergh, aviation pioneer, dies (born 1902). India becomes the sixth nation to explode a nuclear device.

1975 The Xerox corporation releases its computerized typing system with their Diablo printer. Work at Word Processing System (WPS) progresses rapidly at Wang Labs. Chiang Kai-shek dies and is succeeded by his son, Chiang Ching-kuo as the chairman of Kuomintang. North and South Vietnam are united as Socialist Republic of Vietnam with Hanoi as capital. Vietnam War ends.

1976 Dr. Wang introduces the WPS at a New York City trade show. Wang stock begins selling on the American Stock Exchange. Dr. Wang buys land along Route 128 in Lowell, Massachusetts, for expansion of Wang Labs. Chairman Mao Zedong and Premier Zhou Enlai die in China. Thirty high-ranking government and CCP officials are arrested in a coup; Jiang Qing, Mao's widow and the leader of "Gang of Four," is also arrested. Hua Guofeng becomes chairman of the Chinese Communist party. U.S. and U.S.S.R. sign a nuclear arms limitation treaty.

1977 Wang Labs ranks number 32 in the list of the top 50 American computer manufacturers.

1978 Deng Xiaoping initiates agricultural reforms in China.

1979 Many political prisoners are released from Chinese labor camps. China enforces one-couple-one-child policy to curb its population growth. U.S. and China establish diplomatic ties. Margaret Thatcher becomes prime minister of Great Britain. Egypt and Israel sign the Camp David Accord. Islamic fundamentalists, under the leadership of the Ayatollah Ruholla Khomeini, overthrow the shah of Iran. Russian forces invade Afghanistan.

1980 Ronald Reagan, a Republican, is elected president of the U.S.

1981 Wang Labs is listed as the 11th largest American computer manufacturer.

1982 Total sales of Wang Labs amount to $1.1 billion. IBM introduces its famous PC, or Personal Computer. According to the 1982 Chinese census, China's population reaches 1 billion. Nixon visits China to commemorate tenth anniversary of reinstatement of U.S.-Chinese relations. Argentina attempts to seize the Falkland Islands, but is defeated in air, sea, and land battles by Great Britain.

1983 Dr. Wang retires as the president of the Wang Labs. Wang Labs announce development of 14 new products. Chinese government launches a campaign to restrict foreign (Western) culture and morality.

1984 Dr. Wang is listed as the fifth-richest person in the United States with a personal wealth of $1.6 billion. Several industrial reforms are introduced in China.

1985 The Professional Image Computer of Wang Labs is introduced in the market. Mikhail Gorbachev becomes leader of the former Soviet Union; he puts forward plans to change government through *perestroika* (reconstruction) and *glasnost* (openness).

1986 An Wang is presented the Medal of Liberty by President Ronald Reagan. Work force at the Wang Laboratories is reduced to 31,000. Frederick Wang becomes president of Wang Labs. The former Soviet leader Gorbachev calls for better Chinese-Soviet relations. Chinese university students march to advocate democracy, human rights, and freedom.

1987 Portugal and China sign an agreement to return the Portuguese colony of Macao to China in 1999. The Dalai Lama gives a speech for Tibetan independence before U.S. Congress. Martial law is lifted in Taiwan after 39 years of military dictatorship. Pro-independence demonstration takes place in the Tibetan capital city of Lhasa.

1988 Dr. Wang is inducted into the National Inventors Hall of Fame. Chiang Ching-kuo, president of the Republic of China on Taiwan dies; he is succeeded by Lee Teng-hui. Sixteen Tibetan monks are killed in pro-independence riots. China relaxes its one-couple-one-child policy, allowing rural families to have a second child if the first one is a girl. George Bush is elected president of the United States.

1989 Wang Laboratories loses $424 million for the fiscal year. Dr. Wang has an operation for throat cancer; he returns to day-to-day operations of Wang Labs. Frederick Wang resigns as the president of Wang Labs; management of Wang Labs is turned over to Richard Miller. Communism is rejected by country after country in Eastern Europe. The Berlin Wall is officially demolished.

1990 An Wang dies of throat cancer on March 24. East and West Germany are united as Federal Republic of Germany. Mrs. Thatcher resigns as prime minister of Great Britain.

INDEX—Page numbers in boldface type indicate illustrations.

AES, 99
Aiken, Howard, 33, 35-36, 38, 44, 47, **58**, 65
Allegheny Ludlum Steel, 49
Apple computers, 109
Atari computers, 109
Automatic Sequence Controlled Calculator, 33
bankruptcy, of Wang Laboratories, 11
BASIC (Beginner's All-Purpose Symbolic Instruction Code), 89-90, 91, 93
Benrus Time Fellowship, 32
bytes, 50
calculator, electronic, 76-83
cathode ray screen (CRT), 73-74
Chaffee, E. Leon, 32, 35, **56**
Chiang Kai-shek, 17
Chiao Tung University, 21, 22-23, 24, 30, 31
China: Age of Confusion in, 16, 21; and Chiang Kai-shek, 17; civil war in, 31, 33; and Communist takeover, 17-18; Nationalists in, 18, 22, 27; Opium War in, 23; revolution of Sun Yat-sen in, 15; rule of Ch'ing Dynasty in, 15-16; spheres of influence in, 16-17; and war with Japan, 19, 22-27
Chinese-American program, 26-27, 30-31
Ch'ing Dynasty, 15
chips, 70
Chou, Harry, 103
Commodore computers, 109
Communists, 17-18, 22, 27, 33
Compugraphic, 74-75, 79
computerized typewriter, 94
computers, 89; early technology in, 36-37; EDSAC, 45; ENIAC, 36, 39, **58**; magnetism for memory storage, 38; Mark I, 33-34, 36;

Mark III, **60**; Mark IV, 40; matrix wiring, 62-64; Model 700, 91-92; Model 2200, 93; Model 3000, 93; Model 3300 Basic, 90-91; Model 4000, 90; storing information in, 36-38; and typesetting, 73; UNIVAC, 45, **58**
computer chips, 34
computer memory, 44, 46, 48, 49, 90, 92
Confucianism, 19
core memory, 40, 46, 48, 62, 90, 92; sale of patent of, to IBM, 67
CPU (central processing unit), 37, 38, 39
Cunningham, John, 103, 112, 113
Datamation, 106
Deltamax cores, 48-49, 51
Diablo printer, 99
digital electronics, 50
Digital Equipment Corporation (DEC), 90
digital tachometer, 51
Dukakis, Michael, 12
Eckert, J. Presper, 36, 45, **58**
EDSAC (Electronic Discrete Sequential Automatic Computer), 45
electronic calculator, 31, 76-83, 84, 87, 88, 92
ENIAC (Electronic Numerical Integrator and Computer), 36, 39, **59**
exponent, 77
ferrite memory core, 63, 64, 92
ferrites, 48
fluxes, 39
Forrester, Jay W., 41, 46, 63
French concession, in Shanghai, 23, 24
Gallo, Bob, 51
Garth, William, 74
Grayson, Ed, 103

124

Guber, Phillip, 83
Harvard University, 30, 31, 33, 114;
Computation Laboratory at, 33-42,
44-45, 62
Hewlett-Packard, HP 95LX
computer, **59**; 9100 series of
calculators, 91
Hodge, James C., 71
IBM (International Business
Machines), 9; deal with Wang Labs,
13, 14, 62, 64-68; development of
mainframes by, 90; development
of Mark I by, 33; development
of personal computer, 109-113;
development of Selectrics by,
95-96, 99; products manufactured
by, 61-62; purchase of An Wang's
patent by, 64-68; relationship with
Wang Labs, 13, 54, 61-62; response
of, to Wang's computerized
typewriter, 94
integrated circuits, 34, 70, 89, 92
Intel Corporation, 92
international settlement, in
Shanghai, 23, 24
Japan, war with China, 19, 22-27
Jiao Tong University, 21
justification, 73
Kemeny, John, 89
Kirkpatrick, Martin, 62, 65-66, 69
Koplow, Harold, 99
Kun San, 15, 17
Kurtz, Tom, 89
Kweilin, 25-27
Lesnick, Ed, 80, 95
Lessons (Wang), 16, 19-20, 36, 53
Linasec, 74-75
LOCI, 79
logarithms, 77-79
Logiblocs, 71
logic cards, 70, 71
magnetic flux, 39

magnetic memory core, 64. *See also*
core memory
magnetism, 38
mainframes, 90
Mark I computer, 33-35, 36, 39
Mark III computer, **60**
Mark IV computer, 40, 45
Masi, Carl, 101, 102
Massachusetts Institute of
Technology (MIT), 63
mass storage devices, 37-38
matrix, 41, 63-64
matrix wiring, 63
Mauchly, John W., 36, 45, **58**
McCarthyism, 68
Medal of Liberty Award, 12
Mercury delay systems, 38
microcomputers, 109
Miller, Richard, 10, 11, 13
minicomputers, 90
Monroe, 80
Moros, David, 88, 99, 105
Napier, John, 77, 78
Napier's bones, 77
NASA, 42
National Inventors Hall of Fame, 12
Nationalists, 18, 22, 27
Neumann, John von, 45
Newsweek, 85
Olivetti, 80
Opium War, 23
patents, 13, 44, 61, 62, 64, 66-67
Price Waterhouse, Inc., 11
printed circuit boards, 70-71
Professional Image Computer, 112, 113
random access memory (RAM), 37,
38, 41, 64, 92
read only memory (ROM), 37, 92
Reagan, Ronald, 12
Selectric typewriters, 95-96
Shanghai, 15-17, 19, 20-27, 43
Shea Stadium, 71

125

sole proprietorship, 47
stored-program technique of
    computer control, 45
Sun Yat-sen, 15
Syntopican, 101
Tandy computers, 109
Tewksbury, Massachusetts, 76
three-dimensional matrix, 63
toroid, 40, 48
transistors, 69-70
two-dimensional matrix, 63
typesetting advances, 73-75
UNIVAC (Universal Automatic
    Computer), 45, **58**
Victor comptometer, 80
Viehe, Frederick W., 66-67
Vydec, 99
Wang, An: birth of, 12, 15, 47;
    arrival in U.S., 12, 29; education
    of, 12, 18-23, 30-33; and start-up
    of Wang Labs, 12, 47-54; wealth
    of, 12, 68, 82, 85, 87, 88, 113;
    business skills, 12, 50, 54, 82-83;
    death of, 12, 13; as recipient of
    Medal of Liberty, 12; induction of,
    into National Inventors Hall
    of Fame; 12; relationship with
    IBM, 13; legacy of, 13, 114-115;
    patents awarded to, 13, 44, 61, 62,
    64-65, 66-67; childhood of, 15,
    17-20; meaning of name, 15;
    autobiography of, 16, 19-20, 36, 53;
    move of family to Kun San, 17-18;
    return to Shanghai, 20; as soccer
    player, 21; and death of mother, 21;
    as university teacher, 24; and
    project to build radio transmitter,
    25-26; life in Kweilin, 25-27; and
    death of father, 26; as part of the
    Chinese-American program, 26-27,
    30-31; life at Georgetown
    University, 30; trip to Canada, 32;
    postgraduate work of, at Harvard,
    31, 32-33; English skills of, 31;
    as Benrus Time fellow, 32; decision
    to stay in U.S., 33; work at
    Harvard Computation Laboratory,
    33-42, 44-45, 48; invention of core
    memory by, 38-42, 44, 48; marriage
    of, 43; move to Cambridge, 43;
    and birth of son, Frederick, 46-47;
    and pronunciation of name, 47;
    marketing skills of, 48-49; and
    work in digital electronics, 50-51;
    and development of digital
    tachometer, 51; hiring of assistant
    by, 51; exhibit by at the Institute
    of Radio Engineering convention
    booth, 51; work habits of, 52-53;
    relationship with IBM, 54;
    purchase of Boston home by, 61;
    and deal with IBM, 62, 64, 65-66,
    68; as U.S. citizen, 68; birth of son,
    Courtney, 69; and development of
    printed circuit, 70; sale of stock
    to Warner and Swasey, 71-72;
    work of, with Compugraphics,
    74-75; and development of
    electronic calculator, 76-81;
    math knowledge of, 78-79; and
    birth of daughter, Juliette, 82; as
    "the Doctor," 82-83; decision to go
    public with Wang Labs, 82-86;
    family life of, 87; and purchase of
    summer home in Woods Hole,
    Massachusetts, 87; and use of
    chauffeur, 87; prejudice against,
    87-88; and sense of timing, 88;
    decision to enter computer
    business, 89-93; and marketing of
    computerized typewriter, 94-96;
    and development and marketing
    of user friendly word processing
    systems, 99-103, 105, 106-107; and

issuing of new stock class, 103-105; and expansion of corporate headquarters, 106; on IBM, 107; retirement of, 111-112; return to office operations, 113

Wang, An (illustrations): **4; 8; 28;** childhood home of, **55;** family genealogy of **55; 56; 57; 60; 98; 108; 118**

Wang, Courtney (son): **57;** birth of, 69; **108**

Wang, Juliette (daughter): **57;** birth of, 82

Wang, Frederick (son): **8;** as president of Wang Labs, 14; 113-114; as member of board of directors, 14; birth of, 46-47; **57;** employment of, at Wang Labs, 96-97; education of, 96; as head of sales for word processing system, 103; **108;** resignation of, from Wang Labs, 114

Wang, Hsu (sister), **56**

Wang, Lorraine Chiu (wife): marriage of, to An Wang, 43, **57;** move to U.S., 43; move to Cambridge, 43; and birth of son, Frederick, 46-47; as U.S. citizen, 68; and birth of son, Courtney, 69; and birth of daughter, Juliette, 82; wealth of, 87; education of, 87; **108**

Wang, Yin-lu (father), 15, 17-18, 22, **55**

Wang, Z.W. Chien (mother), with sister Z.T., **15**

Wang Center for Performing Arts, 114

Wang Institute of Graduate Studies, 114-115

Wang Laboratories: bankruptcy of, 10-11; becoming a public corporation, 83-86; contract with U.S. air force, 70; Cunningham as president of, 112-113; and development of computerized typewriter, 93-94; and development of Professional Image Computer, 112-113; and development of word processing system, 100-102; earnings of, 52, 75; employment level at, 74, 83, 97; as family company, 48, 69, 84; financial losses of, 10, 95, 113-114; Frederick Wang as president of, 113-114; growth of, 70; incorporation of, 69; and manufacture of electronic calculators, 76-83; and manufacture of printed circuit boards, 69; and marketing of Logiblocs, 70-71; new stock issue by, 101-105; partnership with Compugraphic, 74-75; problems at, 9; products offered by, 10; and purchase of Intel chips, 93; and purchase of Tewksbury property, 76; relationship with IBM, 13, 54, 61-62; sales volume of, 75, 82; start-up of, 12, 47; stock value of, 11, 85-86; and use of IBM Selectrics, 95-96; Warner & Swasey loan to, 71-72; and word processing, 9-10, 94, 100-101

Wang Office, 113

Wang Word Processor, **98**

Warner & Swasey, 71-72

Weditrol (short for Wang Electronic Digital Control Units), 71

Wellesley College, 114

Woods Hole, Massachusetts, 87

word processing, 9, 94, 100-101

World War II, 24, 26-27, 29-30, 34

Xerox, 9, 94, 99

About the Author

Jim Hargrove has worked as a writer and editor for more than ten years. After serving as an editorial director for three Chicago area publishers, he began a career as an independent writer, preparing a series of books for children. He has contributed to works by nearly twenty different publishers. Hargrove has written many titles for Childrens Press, including People of Distinction biographies on Daniel Boone, Diego Rivera, Mark Twain, Martin Sheen, Nelson Mandela, Richard M. Nixon, and Steven Spielberg. He also is the author of *Computer Wars*, which covers the beginning of the computer and the people connected with computers.

DATE			